THE THURSDAY

A Story and Information for Girls Healing From Sexual Abuse.

By PeggyEllen Kleinleder, BSN, RN and Kimber Evensen, LCSW, BCD

Illustrations by Nancy Radtke

THE THURSDAY GROUP: *A Story and Information for Girls Healing from Sexual Abuse*
Copyright © 2009
PeggyEllen Kleinleder and Kimber Evensen
Illustrations Copyright © 2009 Nancy Radtke

Published by:
NEARI Press
70 North Summer Street
Holyoke, MA 01040
413-540-0712

Distributed by:
Whitman Distribution
10 Water Street
P.O. Box 1220
Lebanon, NH 02766
888-632-7412
ISBN# 978-1-929657-44-5

To Crystal and Jon, and all of us who struggle to be true friends to ourselves.

In memory of Carol Demientieff

PeggyEllen

To the little girl I could have been and the little girl I really was. And to all the people who have helped me to understand who I am, put this issue into perspective, and allowed me to see into their healing process. I have been honored beyond words.

Kimber

Contents

V

Our Thanks

From PeggyEllen:

I am deeply grateful to my daughter, Crystal, and son, Jon, for their courage and love. They inspired me to find a format acceptable to young people. My husband, Rich, from the beginning, has seen how much this project means to me and provided encouragement and support. His love for me is unconditional. Kimber Evensen is the best co-author I could ever have dreamed of. My mother, Arlayne Knox, has been my most enthusiastic cheerleader. Carol Demientieff's passionate care and concern for young people reached across time and death to support this book. Bill Schoder-Ehri and Vicky Gordon's wisdom and insight helped this project take shape and find its place in the world. Barton Sloan and Vicky Gordon have helped me remember to breathe. Elizabeth Scollan Watney spoke some of the reassuring words that come out of Carol's mouth in the story, at times when I needed to hear them. Diana Conway's thoughtful comments and nudges over many years helped me stay on track and keep writing. I am grateful to my friends who have listened, loved, and taught me how to be a friend to myself.

From Kimber:

First and foremost, to PeggyEllen, who approached me with a story she had nurtured for over ten years, and who trusted me enough to ask me to be a part of her story telling process. Little can be more important in this world. To my husband, Chris Evensen, who taught me that real love means never giving up and never letting go. No matter how mean and sorry I get, he always loves me and always sees me as a whole, beautiful, and loving person. To my parents, Dick and Cathy, and my

1

children, Gunnar and Nora, who have given me the gifts of history and hope, and to whom I am eternally grateful. To those people who have helped to shape me as a person and as a professional, and who remain a part of my thoughts and behaviors as a therapist, including Dr. Roger Graves, Dr. Joseph Sonderliter, "Dr. Bob" Morgan, and Jim Miller. With special thanks and untold gratitude to Val Miraglia, Mark Nelles, Randee Shafer, and Renee Raferty, without whom I would be less of a person, and less of a therapist. You have taught me to trust in my conviction that to truly connect with others in a real and human manner is the only way in which a person can make any difference in the lives of those they treat. To become real, one must love and be loved. And in memory of my friends, my colleagues, Alice Abraham, one of the best therapists I have known, and John Michaud, who had more courage than most. But especially, and most importantly, to the people who remain in my thoughts, prayers, and hopes for the future; those whom I have worked with closely enough to have learned their innermost thoughts, wishes, and horror. I often think on the difference between those who are obvious heroes in the eyes of the public, and those who are heroes in the quietest of ways. The bravery and courage it must take to save the life of another human being while risking your own must be a terrifying and exciting experience, and one that we all acknowledge as amazing. But it is those who brave their own fears, who have the courage to save themselves, to tell their own story, and who choose to fight with themselves to live, for whom I have the greatest respect and awe. I am a therapist because as such, I am privileged to see the kind of courage that almost no one would risk sharing out loud. I admire courage that faces a whole world of people who can rarely see or acknowledge the pain and bravery that they have faced, a world of people, who, if anything, greet them with contempt, disbelief, ignorance, misunderstanding, or fear. I honor the everyday heroes in my life, those who are among the very bravest and most admirable of people I know. My clients.

OUR THANKS

From both of us:

Nancy Radtke's enthusiasm for this project was clear from the moment we asked her to participate. She carefully crafted her illustrations with few details, to invite readers to add to the drawings in their minds or with their pens, making the book more personally meaningful.

It has been wonderful to have the opportunity to work with the team at NEARI Press. Their dedication to healing the complicated problem of sexual abuse is clear in all their interactions. Euan Bear's insightful, patient, and encouraging editing has been a true gift.

We are indebted to all of those who read this manuscript in its many versions and gave us valuable comments and encouragement, including Paul Ginter, Rob Longo, Leona (Kokie) Schick, Val Miraglia, Diane Payne, Julia Perez, Nancy Radke, Diana Conway, Vicky Gordon, Bill Schoder-Ehri, Elizabeth Scollan Watney, Elizabeth Spanuello, Arlayne Knox, Laurie Holland Klein, Heather McIntyre, Adrienne Dewey, Rachel Kacshur, David R. Klein, Laurentia Chamblee, Maya Rohr, Margaret O'Connor, Louis Lehmann, Amy Bollenbach, Anne X. Doerpinghaus, Patty Swanson, Joanne Uppendahl, Wendy Noomah, Clara Noomah, Claudia Ehli, Elsie Eckman, Sue Dean, Jo Going, and many others who chose to remain anonymous.

Hello Reader,

My name is Abigail, or Abi for short. I am 13 years old and I live in a small town in Alaska. This is a book about some things that happened when I was in sixth grade and how I ended up learning more about dealing with hard feelings than I ever imagined I would need. My whole purpose in writing this is because I want something good to come out of all that confusion and weirdness. I don't want anyone to feel as lonely as I did. This book is partly about what happened to me and to the girls I met in my support group (they all gave me permission to share their stories with you), but it is mostly about the things we learned and did afterwards that helped us heal. I didn't include too many details about the actual sexual abuse experiences, because that can be really hard to read if you've been abused yourself.

You might be reading this book because someone you know has been sexually abused or you might be reading it because you've been sexually abused yourself. Either way, you could still have some uncomfortable, difficult, or scary feelings about what happened. Reading about other people's feelings might make your own feelings about the abuse come to the surface, which can feel overwhelming. Try to read little bits of this book at a time. My therapist suggests that it is best to read this sort of thing during the day, rather than at night or before you go to bed. And it's a good idea to have someone you trust in the house with you or near you while you are reading, in case you start to have big feelings. Try not to get so lost in the story that you forget to notice your own body and brain. If you start to notice that your breathing becomes uneven or really fast, or your heart feels like it is pounding in your chest or you get dizzy or feel unreal – please, put the book down, look at the things that are around you, and go find or call that trusted adult. (If you don't have an adult in your life that you can talk to, you can call Child Help USA. Their number is **1-800-4ACHILD**, or **1-800-422-4453**. The call is free and it won't show up on your regular phone bill, but it will show up on a cell phone bill). Other reasons for putting the book down or taking a break and talking to someone, are having strong memories or flashbacks of the abuse, panic feelings, feeling as if you are outside of your own body, or noticing a major change in your eating habits. And if you have any thoughts about hurting or killing yourself, or feeling like you need to drink or use drugs, believe me, those are sure signs that your feelings are getting too big to handle on your own! These are all ways that your body and your brain are telling you that they are on overload.[1] These defenses are ways people try to cope with strong feelings. Even though they can feel weird and scary, strong feelings are totally normal and expected considering what you have been through. Give yourself a break, put the book down for a while, and go relax, exercise, or do something fun.

Recovering from abuse can be hard work. You may want to ignore it and try to get on with your life or to push yourself to heal really fast, but my therapist says that it's important to take it slowly and to really talk about all the feelings you're having. She says you can't get past the past unless you deal with it. If you have been abused, I hope that you will find a therapist or counselor to work with, or talk to yours if you already have one. It is best if you can read this book while you are meeting with a therapist, so that you can talk to him or her about your responses when you get together.

Before we get started, I want to tell you about the different parts of this book. First, there is my story itself. Along with the story you will find more facts and information that I got from my group leader and my therapist and stuff I looked up on the Internet. In the back of the book is a Glossary for words I didn't know or wasn't sure about before all of this happened, and a sort of handbook of more stuff you or your parents might need to know. If you have questions about a certain thing, look at the Index in the very back of the book. Hopefully, that will make it easier to find what you need. Feel free to jump around and read what interests you. Everybody is different and what is helpful to one person might not be what another person needs at all.

I am a fictional character, but I was created out of the very real feelings and experiences of the girls PeggyEllen and Kimber used to be, and the girls they have known.

We hope that this book will help you heal.

Abi, PeggyEllen, & Kimber

Chapter 1

What Is Normal, Anyway?

A year and a half ago, five minutes into my sixth grade math class at Bluff K-12 School, my average little life began to fall apart. It started innocently enough. A student office runner came in and handed a yellow note to the teacher. She frowned and then asked me to go to the office.

"Try not to miss the whole period, Abi. We're reviewing for Friday's test."

"Nice of her to broadcast to the whole sixth grade class how stupid I am in math," I grumbled under my breath as I followed the runner back to the office. I was wondering if it was another mix-up about transferring my school records up here to Alaska from my school in California. I didn't get nervous until I walked into the school counselor's tiny office and saw both my mother and the principal squeezed into kindergartener sized chairs next to each other.

The counselor offered me an itty bitty orange chair and then glanced at my mother. My mother answered him with a tense little shake of her head. Too upset to speak. Bad sign. The counselor took a deep breath and opened his mouth.

"You will need to go up to the Hospital with your mother, Abigail," the principal blurted. "They will explain everything to you up there," she said, standing up abruptly. The counselor looked confused.

"Is Dad hurt?" I shrieked, jumping out of my chair, my stomach lurching into my throat and then dropping down again when my mother shook her head at me.

"No, no, no," the counselor said in a soothing voice. "Please sit down, Abi." He turned to the principal.

"I'll talk with them," he said quietly. "It's okay. I'll brief you afterwards." I felt like I was going to explode.

"What's going on?" I whispered to my mom through clenched teeth, as the principal slipped out, looking relieved. Mom opened her mouth but she couldn't seem to find the words and this time it was the counselor who jumped in. He said that the youth pastor at my church was being investigated for sexual behavior with children and that the police had found pictures in his apartment that appeared to be child pornography.

Some of the pictures were of me. I could feel my face getting hot and my brain didn't seem to be working very well. Sexual behavior? Child pornography? I wasn't even sure what pornography meant, just that it was bad. I was wearing clothes the whole time. Phil told me he was taking pictures for a friend who had a modeling company. The counselor explained that the police wanted to interview me at the hospital.

What Kind of People Abuse?

People who sexually abuse children come from all ethnic and racial groups. They can be male or female, rich or poor, homosexual or heterosexual, married or single[1].

I sure didn't think Phil would turn out to be a criminal! Abi

What Is Sexual Abuse?

Child sexual abuse can include both physical contact and non-physical contact. There are different definitions for sexual abuse, but they all come down to the same thing. It is wrong for adults or teenagers to be sexual with children. It is wrong and it is the older person's responsibility to stop it from happening. No grownup has the right to be sexual with a child, ever, no matter what their relationship with that child.

I got my coat and boots from my locker and my mother drove me up to the hospital. She was wearing her robot-mom face and she kept starting to ask me things in an angry tone of voice and then stopping herself.

"What were you…."

"How could you have…"

I had questions too, but it didn't seem like a particularly good time. The hospital was on a big open bluff overlooking the river. We hurried from the car, huddling against the wind and snow. A tall woman met us at the door. She helped us pull the door shut and smiled at me. "Dreadful out, isn't it? You must be Abigail. I'm Elaine, your advocate from Women's Resources."

She said that her job was to help and support me. Part of me felt like saying "Whatever," but I didn't. She took us to a room that looked like a doctor's office except for the basket of dolls and stuffed animals in the corner. While we waited there she told us that a nurse and a cop would be asking me questions about what happened with Phil, and then the nurse would give me a physical exam. She said that if I felt uncomfortable with anything that was happening in the interview I should speak up and let them know. I was about to ask why they would have to examine me since Phil barely even touched me, when the nurse and police officer showed up. My mother had to wait in the next room while they talked to me. They were tape recording the whole thing.

I told them about how Phil had said he was going to send the pictures to a modeling company. His closet was full of gorgeous outfits. He kept encouraging me to put on different ones and do sexy poses. I didn't tell them everything. I didn't tell them he said that I was "stunning," or that I knew some of the fancy outfits were way too skimpy. He was always really polite and only touched me occasionally, like when he was adjusting a strap on my shoulder or helping with a zipper. I didn't tell them I felt kind of uncomfortable about it, but I didn't want to stop because it was exciting and fun. Sometimes I imagined I was practicing to be on MTV. It felt like a weird thing to be doing with a youth pastor, but I never thought of it as sexual abuse. It started out not weird at all, and at first he never touched me.

After they asked a lot of questions, the cop wanted me to let the nurse examine me, to see if Phil had left any marks on me. It was like they didn't believe me that he had barely touched me. I told them I didn't want to take my clothes off. They showed me a stupid little video with puppets in it about how the exam wasn't any big deal. The nurse tried to convince me she just wanted to make sure I was okay. When I kept saying no, they finally gave up.

Myth: It wasn't abuse unless there was sexual intercourse or force was used.

Fact: People who offend sexually use many tricky behaviors to trap or lure kids into situations they can't control. Some of the tricks include threats, pressure, bullying, lies, bribes, and grooming (saying and doing things specifically meant to make you feel comfortable around them so that you are easier to abuse later). They may do this in person, or even over the internet in chat rooms.

My mom told my father about it as soon as he got home from work. I could make out the swear words he was shouting even though my bedroom is upstairs and I had my door shut. I couldn't face him. That was the first Worst Day of My Life (WDOML #1).

WDOML #2 was the next week, after the Bluff weekly newspaper had an article about Phil and all the things he was accused of doing. Even though my name wasn't in the article, somehow everybody seemed to know I was involved. I guess that's what happens in a small town, but it sure took me by surprise.

The other thing that shocked me was that kids were saying that Jessica Cornfield was the person who had told on him. They said that she had gone to the school counselor and told him that Phil had been molesting her. The school counselor called the police.

A Physical Exam

When sexual abuse includes touching or having sex, it can leave tiny marks, tears, or other signs on a person's body. If you were touched under your clothing during sexual abuse, you may be asked to have a physical exam.

If you want to read more about physical exams you can look on page 206. Abi

How Can You Get Help When You've Been Abused?

Since there are rarely any physical signs of sexual abuse, there may be no way of getting help without actually telling someone about the abuse. Even when a therapist, social worker, or police officer suspects sexual abuse, it isn't something that they can address well without hearing it directly from the person who was abused. This is a heavy and unfair burden. If you have been abused, it would be natural to feel angry* about the whole situation. Not only were you abused, but, now to get help healing, you have to get up the nerve to tell someone about it!

or confused or ashamed... Abi

What If You Can't Say It Out Loud or Aren't Believed?

It is hard work to tell about being abused. Many people who have been abused never tell at all. You are reading this book, so most likely you have already told someone. Whoever you told, you did a good and brave thing. If you have not yet told an adult, sometimes drawing, singing, or running it out can help get around the words that can get stuck in your throat. If you tell and aren't believed, keep telling until someone believes you and helps you. You deserve that help and belief. If you don't want to talk to someone in person, you can call Child Help USA. Their number is **1-800-4ACHILD**, or **1-800-422-4453**. The call is free and it won't show up on your regular phone bill (but it will show up on a cell phone bill). The person who answers your call can help you to find the right people to help you.

The thing is, at the time I despised Jessica. She was a big girl (I thought of her as fat back then), with stringy blond hair. She was always curled around a book or writing in her notebook. Every time she laughed, which she would do if anybody tried to talk to her, her hand flew up to cover her mouth. She was sort of friendly to me at church when I first moved to Bluff, but I was pretty cold toward her. I didn't really want to be associated with her. On WDOML #2 it seemed like every whispered conversation featured Jessica and me. I wanted to die.

A lot has happened since that day. I stopped numbering the worst days (after WDOML #25). It hasn't all been bad. I don't hate Jessica anymore. I certainly don't hate Alaska anymore. I don't even hate myself anymore. I wish I could go back in time and tell my sixth grade self the things I know now. That's why I'm writing this book. I want something good to come out of all that mess. I can't fix what happened, but maybe what I learned could help someone else.

Maybe other girls won't have to feel quite so lonely and confused, if they read about all my weird thoughts and feelings. I've been doing a lot of writing anyway, because writing stuff down helps me figure out what I'm feeling and sometimes even why.

I'm no expert, but there are facts along with the story in case you want more information about certain things. Some are handouts from the group I was in, and some are things I looked up, or found out from my therapist. In the back of the book is a glossary for any words you don't understand. One of the most important things I learned is that I am a whole and complete person. I have a core self inside, even though I didn't used to believe it. When I am caring and compassionate toward myself and others, I am acting from that part of me – my truest self. I still have parts that get triggered by memories of the abuse, or by other people's stories of abuse. At times I need help from my therapist when I get overwhelmed by the parts of myself that are still angry or scared. My smallest (youngest) and most vulnerable parts want to run away and hide sometimes, but I have learned how to protect them and be a true friend to myself.

The Importance of Telling

Telling someone about sexual abuse is scary. You wonder how they will react and what will happen afterwards. But living with the memories and feelings about sexual abuse can continue to hurt you. If you haven't told about being abused, think about people you could tell. Perhaps you have a friend or family member, a teacher, or a priest who cares about you and who is a good listener. It is okay to say: "Could I please talk with you privately?"

Chapter 2

. . . .

Grand Jury

Five weeks after the police interview at the hospital I had to be a witness at Phil's Grand Jury Hearing. It seemed like a long time to wait, but later I found out that people sometimes have to wait months before Grand Jury happens. The Grand Jury is group of 18 adults who listen to information about what happened and decide whether there is enough information and evidence to have an actual trial. We drove to Anchorage because Bluff isn't big enough to have a Grand Jury. Elaine from Women's Resources rode with us. Mom had the heater blasting the whole way. She forced me to wear warm clothes because it was below zero. She always thinks the worst is going to happen, like the car breaking down. She is still like that. I took my parka off but I roasted

You Have Legal Rights

- You have the right not to be abused.
- You have the right to know when all court dates are scheduled, and every time they are changed.
- You have the right to complete a "victim impact statement" (stating how the abuser's behavior has affected you) to be read out loud to the court.
- You have the right not to speak to the person who abused you.
- You have the right not to speak to the lawyer who represents the person who abused you (unless you are testifying in court).

For more information about legal stuff, look on page 201. Abi.

anyway. Elaine told us what to expect. She said they would ask the witnesses to come in one at a time to the courtroom. Phil and his attorney would not be there, just the District Attorney, a court record keeper, and the 18 people on the jury. She said there would be three other girls as witnesses.

"I thought he was just doing stuff with me and Jessica." I said.

Elaine shook her head. "After the newspaper article came out about Phil molesting children, two other girls told their parents that Phil had been touching them sexually." I wanted to hear the details, but Elaine said that information was not public.

"How come it wasn't in the newspaper?" I asked. It gave me a creepy feeling to hear about the other girls getting molested. I wondered what Phil would have tried to get me to do next, if Jessica hadn't told on him.

"There may be an article next week," Elaine said.

"Why do you want to know so much about it?" my mother asked.

"I don't," I said.

"Questions are okay." Elaine said. Nobody said anything. You could hear the hum of the studded snow tires on the pavement. Eventually, my mom and Elaine started talking about where they wanted to go shopping in Anchorage if we had time after Grand Jury.

Shame, Secrecy, and Isolation

Sexual abuse is a form of abuse that usually happens in secrecy and isolation. Only about 10 percent of children who have been abused ever tell an adult about it.[1] Many people never tell. Since sex and sexual abuse are both difficult subjects to talk about, and since abusers often use shaming to keep their victims quiet, most people suffer in silence after being abused. You can get help. Call **1-800-4ACHILD** or **1-800-422-4453**. *You don't have to be alone.*

When we got to the Anchorage courthouse a friendly looking man in a suit and a Mickey Mouse tie met us in the hallway. He said he was Alex, the Victim Witness Coordinator. He led us into a private room and explained about the hearing. Most of what he told us we had already heard from Elaine on the way up. He said what happened in Grand Jury was private and it was against the law to talk about it outside the Court House. My mother asked if he meant that afterwards we couldn't talk about Phil to anyone.

"No," Alex said, "You and Abigail and her dad may need to talk with people you trust. Talking with others helps you to heal from the abuse. It is just that you aren't to talk about what the District Attorney asks or tells you, and the people on the Grand Jury are not allowed to mention anything about what you or any of the other witnesses say." That was fine with me. I didn't want any more people to know about how stupid I had been. The District Attorney knocked on the door and then clicked quickly into the room with her high heels and skirt suit. As soon as she had smiled and introduced herself, she rushed out.

Who Abuses?

Mothers	People who are thought of as Elders
Fathers	
Sisters	Foster parents
Brothers	Babysitters
Aunts	Cousins
Uncles	Rabbis
Stepparents	Priests
Grandparents	Youth Pastors & Ministers
Police officers	
Family friends	Coaches
Teachers	Doctors
Counselors & Therapists	Tribal leaders
	Strangers

Sheeesh! Abi

If You Have to Go to Court

You can ask your guardian ad litem or victim's advocate to take you to visit the courthouse or courtroom before the hearing or trial so that you can get a feel for what things look like and where you or other people will be in the courtroom.

You can wear whatever you want to court. You don't have to be dressed up. Wear something you'll feel comfortable in. You can bring your favorite stuffed animal, wear "power jewelry" (like a bracelet or necklace that helps you to feel powerful or confident), or bring something to hold in your hands while you testify.

For more information about going to court, look on page 203. Abi

We went back out in the hallway and waited around while Jessica and the two other girls talked with the Victim Witness Coordinator. I wished my dad had come instead of my mom. Her face was hard and blank. I couldn't tell what she was thinking. Maybe she was wishing she didn't have such a stupid, slutty kid for a daughter. At least with my dad, I know what he's thinking. I found out he had been yelling about killing Phil, not me, that night of WDOML #1. The next morning when he talked to me about what happened he didn't act mad at me, more like disappointed and hurt. He hated Phil for "taking advantage" of my "innocence," was the way he put it.

After everyone talked to Alex, the Victim Witness guy, we went one by one into the courtroom. When it was finally my turn to go in, I felt numb. The District Attorney asked me questions like the ones the cop had asked me. A few people on the Grand Jury asked questions, too. It was weird, because it was almost like I was watching myself give the answers.

The Grand Jury decided there was enough evidence to have a trial. What I couldn't understand was why Phil was saying he wasn't guilty even though there were pictures. The advocate said maybe he was hoping his lawyer would find a way to keep the pictures out of the trial. Secretly, I hoped they would keep the pictures out, because I didn't want everybody to see them.

Chapter 3

Waiting for the Trial

My family had moved from California to Bluff just a few months before I started doing the modeling stuff with Phil. There were kids at school that I'd started to talk to, but I was just the new girl from California to them. They didn't really know me. After they heard about the sexual abuse some of them acted weird to me.

Jake, a boy that I'd sort of liked, made a joke about my modeling career. I kept to myself after that. I hated acting like Jessica the Outcast, but I guess my self-esteem was shot. There was always a part of me watching myself from the outside. Finally, school got out for the summer, but the trial still hadn't happened. I begged my parents to let me go back to California and spend the summer at my grandparents, my dad's family. To my huge surprise, they let me. They said they'd just bring me back early if the trial happened. All summer long, nobody said anything about what had happened in Bluff. There were hours, days even, when I forgot it had ever happened.

For laws and information about sexual abuse in all 50 states, as well as Federal guidelines, look up Susan Smith's Legal Resources for Victims of Sexual Abuse at www.smith-lawfirm.com or Tribal Law and Policy Institute at www.tlpi.org

What Is Consent Anyway?

A person consents (agrees) to sexual contact when they want to participate in kissing, touching, or other sexual acts and they clearly let that desire be known to the other person. If a person says "no", it does not matter that they said "yes" yesterday, or if they will say "yes" again tomorrow. It doesn't matter if they are your girlfriend, boyfriend, or even if you are married to them. It doesn't matter if they said "yes" two seconds ago; if they say "no" NOW, then you have to stop because you no longer have consent.

In order to consent to sexual activity, a person has to agree to the specific act at the specific time. If the person says "yes" to one thing, or fifty things, it doesn't mean that they are saying, or will say, "yes" to any other sexual behavior.

A person who is under the age of legal consent (which varies from state to state and can be anywhere between 16 and 18 years old in the U.S.) or who is drunk, or drugged, or who does not have the intellectual ability needed to be able to consent to sexual acts, is not legally able to consent (agree) to sex acts. To find out the age of consent in your state, and throughout the world, look up http://www.avert.org/aofconsent.htm

I came back in the fall, all tan with sun-blonde hair and more homesick for California than ever. I hated being in seventh grade. When I saw other kids laughing and talking with each other, I was afraid they were talking about me. I was never great in school, but I'd always gotten okay grades before seventh grade. I couldn't concentrate. Worries about the trial and images of what happened with Phil filled up my mind. I felt like I was taken over by some part of myself I had never met before, a spacey, distant, lonely part that protected me from dealing with things happening around me. At home I listened to music a lot. I stopped playing piano. My parents thought I was just mad at them for moving us to Alaska.

That stupid trial kept getting postponed. I kept wondering what it would be like to have to see him again at the trial. Part of me was so angry I felt like Phil might need protection from me. Finally in November for some reason they decided to videotape me answering the lawyer's questions. I hated having to tell the whole story over again in embarrassing detail. In December they said that it had been settled out of court, which meant there wasn't going to be any trial. Phil is in prison now. Sometimes I wonder if he is getting any kind of help for his problem, or what's going to stop him from doing it again to some other girls when he gets out of jail.

Sex Offender Treatment Programs

Sex offender treatment programs look at the way a person who has been convicted of a sex offense thinks and acts. They also address the way that person believes, what his or her values are, and what kinds of habits the person has formed. This type of therapy is designed to change the thinking errors that help the offender excuse, deny, or justify his or her behavior. The therapy will also set up safety plans with people who abuse and their support people in order to reduce the chances that they will behave in a sexually abusive manner again.

For more about treatment programs, look on page 210... Abi

Chapter 4

Maybe I Could Use a Little Support

I moped around through the holidays, but my parents didn't seem to notice. When my grades came out in January that was a different story. Mom and dad met with my teachers. That's when my mother decided that I needed to see a therapist at the Mental Health Center.

I didn't mind talking with Jean. She had modeling clay and little toys, things you could fiddle with or look at while you were talking. It was Jean's idea for me to go to the Support Group for Girls Who Have Been Sexually Abused at the Women's Resource Center. She thought I needed more information about sexual abuse, lots more information. It's true that I had been wondering about certain things. Mostly about what was wrong with me. Jean asked me to write about the group in a notebook, so we could talk about any questions I had. I wasn't thrilled about being in a group with other girls. I tend to get along better with guys; at least I did back then. If I'd known who'd be there, I would've refused to go.

Understanding Therapy

Some people are embarrassed or afraid to go to a therapist. They may believe that therapy is only for "crazy people." The truth is that we all need someone to talk to and to help us through difficult times. If you break your leg or have high blood pressure or diabetes, you go see a medical doctor, and if you have a toothache or a cavity you go see a dentist. Therapists are people who help you through big feelings. They're kind of like a "feelings doctor." There are all kinds of therapists; yours might be called a social worker, a counselor, a psychologist, or a family therapist. Whatever your therapist is called doesn't really matter, as long as he or she is kind and respectful toward you and your family and really understands how to help you.

One snowy day in March, Mom picked me up after school and dropped me off in front of the Women's Resource Center. The receptionist took me down a hallway to the group room. When we got to the doorway and I saw Jessica Cornfield sitting in one of the beanbag chairs, I got an immediate stomachache. I hated being associated with her.

There were five of us in the group and I recognized the three other girls from school. I'd never have guessed that they were sexual abuse victims like me. Even though I knew that I wasn't the only person who had ever been abused, somehow a part of me always felt very alone or different; that part of me didn't really believe that other "normal" people could have been abused. The girls I'd seen at the Grand Jury hearing weren't there. The leader of the group was an Alaska Native woman named Carol. My mom and I had met with her the week before, so at least she wasn't a total stranger.

The first thing she told us in group was about the rules and how the group's supposed to be a safe place. She made a shape with her hands when she said safe, like she was holding a huge ball of air. We weren't supposed to

What Do Therapists Really Do Anyway?

Your therapist is there to help you get in touch with your feelings, express your feelings, and to move into new feelings. Therapists help people to identify old coping patterns that are no longer useful (ways of protecting yourself or walling off others), coping skills that are harmful (drinking alcohol, hurting yourself, stuffing your feelings) and build new, healthy coping skills (learning to calm yourself, feel centered, and accept yourself).

criticize each other and we weren't supposed to talk about what anybody said or did in the group outside the group. I got nervous because that sounded like what Phil said to me about not telling anyone about what we were doing. It actually seemed like a scared part inside of me was getting up and walking out the door of the group room, she was so freaked. Then Carol said she'd be giving us information about sexual abuse and about healing from sexual abuse and she wanted us to feel free to discuss what she said with our parents and friends and therapist or counselor. We just weren't supposed to talk about what the other girls said about themselves. I was glad she explained that. It felt like that scared part of me came back and sat down again.

Is What I Say in Therapy Really Private?

It will help you to feel safe if you know that what you say and do in therapy is confidential. You need to be able to trust that you can share things, or express feelings in ways that will not come back to hurt or embarrass you.

When you are in individual or group counseling, you don't have to keep the information the therapist shares with you private. On the other hand, the therapist is required by laws and by their professional rules to keep what you say private, with only a few exceptions. The exceptions all have to do with protecting your safety and/or the safety of others. If your therapist does ask you to keep something from your individual sessions secret, that's a red flag that something might not be right. Tell someone else about what's going on.

Check with your own therapist if you have any questions about your rights. There is more information about confidentiality on page 200. Abi

THE THURSDAY GROUP: A Story and Information for Girls Healing from Sexual Abuse

After she told us the rules, Carol opened up a blue velvet bag next to her and took out a round gray and white rock almost as big as her hand. "I found this in our river." Our river? I guessed she must mean the Goldhills River that runs through the woods behind the Women's Resource Center and then out of town below the big bluffs. "It is going to be our talking stone." Nobody said anything. "Has anyone used a talking stone before?" Nobody said anything. "Talking circles are used by a number of American Indian tribes. A stone or feather or other natural object is passed around the circle as people talk." I looked over at the girl sitting on the beanbag chair in the corner. She looked Alaska Native, too.

Most of the Native people in Bluff are Athabaskans, which is a kind of Alaska Native but also an Alaskan Indian or something. It is sort of confusing to me. Before I moved to Alaska I thought all of the Alaska Native people were Eskimos.

Myth: Sexual abuse only happens to other people.

Fact: Sexual abuse happens to people of all races and ethnic groups. It happens to males and females, to people who are rich and to people who are poor. It has been around for centuries and, unfortunately, it still happens today.[1]

(Later I found out I had been totally clueless, since after I got to be friends with her, she told me that before white people came here there were actually 20 different languages spoken in Alaska and that there are over 200 different tribes.) She was watching Carol closely. She pushed her glasses up on her nose like she wanted to see better. I wondered if she had heard of talking stones and what she thought about Carol.

"The person who is holding the stone is the person talking. The others in the group listen. If the person holding the stone says it is okay, the others can ask questions to better understand what the person is saying. Otherwise, they just listen. When the talker is finished, she passes it to the next person in the circle. If she does not want to say anything she can pass the stone on silently. Are there any questions?" Nobody said anything.

For the first round, she wanted us to say our names, one thing we liked to do, and one thing we liked about ourselves. She went first. She said one thing she liked to do is walk in the woods with her dog and one thing she liked about herself was her nose. I thought that was weird because her nose is kind of big. There's nothing wrong with it. It's straight and everything. It's just big. Then it was my turn. I said I was Abi, of course, and that I liked to play piano and that I liked my nose, too. Everyone kind of laughed. I was trying to be funny, but I do like my nose. It's a normal looking nose with no freckles and the nostrils point down like they should so people can't see up them like some peoples' noses. Then the black girl sitting next to me said her name was Imaya and she liked running and she couldn't think of anything she liked about herself. I don't know why she said that because she's tall and looks like a model. Her hair was all in tiny braids with beads. Somebody must have spent a lot of time on it.

Then it was Jessica's turn. She turned really red and looked down at the rock so her greasy blonde hair swung forward around her face, and

Isn't Therapy Supposed to Help?
Something you should know about therapy is that it may bring up old stuff that you haven't thought about or dealt with in a long time. That's good because it gives you the chance to work through it. But it can also be scary, because as you begin to do this work, it may seem like things are getting worse, not better. That's because you are starting to think about things that you may have avoided for a long time. As you continue to work through your feelings, though, you will notice that you start to feel better and better.

mumbled something about liking to read. She smiled in an embarrassed way and covered her mouth with her hand. Then she shoved the rock over to the girl who looked Alaska Native. Her name was Tara. She turned it in her hands, exploring the tiny crevices with her fingertips, and then rubbing the smooth parts with her thumb. Her hands looked strong. She didn't have any rings on them or fingernail polish. I wondered if she was going to say anything at all. Finally, in a soft voice, she said she liked to be with animals. The fifth girl's name was Danielle. She was tiny and couldn't sit still. Her thick black hair fell in ringlets down to her shoulders and jiggled when she talked. What she liked to do was play softball and what she liked about herself was being a good pitcher. I thought she was going to say her hair, because I would have, if I had hair like that.

Then we played a game like musical chairs where the person who is standing up says something about herself, for example, "I like to eat chocolate." Then everyone who likes chocolate has to get up and change seats and she tries to grab a seat so someone else is left standing up. Jessica didn't play. That was another of the rules for the group. If you didn't want to participate in an activity you just said, "I pass." I didn't really want to play either, but I didn't want to do the same thing as Jessica. Part of me envied her for being able to sit out. I resented her for doing what I wanted to do, but it ended up being pretty fun in the end.

Chapter 5

It's Too Much!

A week later we had our second support group meeting. We met on Thursdays at four in the Women's Resource building. It's down by the river in the oldest, coldest part of town. Luckily, it was nice and warm inside. There were three old couches and a couple of beanbag chairs in the group room. Nothing matched. The carpet smelled new, but everything else smelled old, like ancient sleeping bags.

After everyone got there, Carol asked if anyone had any questions about the group. Nobody else said anything, so I said I was wondering if only girls and women get sexually abused since it's called Women's Resources not People's Resources and there are only girls in our group. Carol said she could understand how I thought that, but it isn't true. Sometimes the mental health center, across town, has groups for boys that have been abused.

Is it Harder for Boys to Tell?

Boys and men in America are often taught that they should be tough, independent, and able to take care of themselves. People around them sometimes think boys cannot be abused, or that they are not affected as much as girls if they are abused. When they are abused, they often think that they should have done something to stop the abuse, or that what happened to them wasn't abuse. Whether you are a boy or a girl, telling someone about the abuse is much harder when you think that you should have done something to stop it, or that you shouldn't be having strong feelings about it.

For more information about boys who have been abused see page 214. Abi

She said about one in every three or four girls and one in four to six boys get sexually abused before they are 18. It's even more than that in Alaska.[1]

She also said that not all sexual abusers are men. Women also abuse children, both boys and girls. Then we passed the talking stone around and said how we felt about that. I said it made me feel better that I wasn't the only one, but it is weird nobody I knew had ever talked about it. I didn't say it, but I wondered if I knew any boys that had been abused. I had never really thought about sexual abuse very much before. Now it seemed like almost anyone could be abused and almost anyone could be an abuser — even a woman (!).

Tara pushed her glasses up. "I don't know." She shrugged, shook her head, looked down at her lap, and passed.

Jessica just sat there looking at the rock in her hands and finally whispered, "I'm glad there are no guys in our group." Imaya passed the rock to Danielle without saying anything. Danielle's face was so white her freckles looked like they were floating above her skin. Everybody was staring at her except Tara.

"What is it, Danielle?" Carol asked.

Sexual Abuse By Females

Our society has a hard time believing that a woman could sexually abuse a child because we tend to think of women as nurturing caregivers. This can make it even harder for people who have been abused by a woman to talk about or report the abuse. Even though we don't think of women as abusers, studies indicate that up to 40 percent of boys who are abused are abused by women[2]. Women also abuse girls, and sometimes they abuse their own children as well.

For more information about females who abuse, see page 216. Abi

"I didn't know it was so common," Danielle said in a voice as thin as paper. "Does it happen to some people more than once?"

"Yes, it does."

"I wish I hadn't come here," Danielle said. "I wish you hadn't told me that." She hugged her knees and started rocking from side to side. "I couldn't stand to have it happen to me again." She had her head down and all you could see was a pile of curls on top of her knees. Imaya reached out her hand as if she was going to touch Danielle's hair or her shoulder but pulled it back. Maybe she was afraid to make things worse. I wished I hadn't brought this whole thing up.

"Danielle," Carol said, leaning toward her, "it looks as though you are having some of the overwhelming feelings from when you were abused. It will help you feel better to lift your head and look around you. You are safe now. You are with friends. Take a deep breath." I tried to look friendly, but part of me just wanted to get out of there. "Let's all stand up and stomp around a little to remind ourselves where we are." She stood up and started marching around the room. Even Danielle looked up and stared at her like she was crazy.

"I'm serious," Carol laughed, waving her arms, "Everyone up on your feet."

After we all stomped around Danielle looked a lot better.

"I'm sorry. It was just so scary."

"No need to apologize," Carol said. "It's normal to be frightened when a terrifying thing happens to you. Some of the things we talk about in this group are bound to remind you of the abuse and likely to bring back some of the

Grounding and Centering Yourself

You can distract yourself from big feelings and help to center yourself by changing your body position. If you are lying down, sit up. If you are sitting, stand. You can stomp your feet hard on the ground to remind yourself that you are in the present, right here, right now, and not experiencing the past.

feelings from that time. We can help each other with difficult feelings here, and it is also important to talk about those feelings with your therapist."

"But I'm frightened all the time, now." Danielle ran her fingers through her curls so they jiggled in a cloud around her head. "Ever since that man attacked me in my bedroom, it's like it doesn't matter where I am, I'm scared. You know the stories you hear about kids getting kidnapped, or babysitters getting murdered, I'd hear about them, or see something on television, but it never seemed real. Like I never thought anything really bad would happen to me. Now I'm afraid more bad things could happen to me any minute." Suddenly I realized who Danielle was. I had read about her in the newspaper. A man climbed into a girl's bedroom during the night. He threatened the girl with a knife and did something to her. They called it sexual assault in the 2nd degree in the newspaper. Finally, her brother woke up and scared the man off.

I was shocked. That was much worse sexual abuse than what had happened to me. A new awful feeling ran through me. How would she feel if she knew I had a choice about what happened to me? How would she feel about being in a group with me?

"Not all sexual abuse is as bad as what happened to you," I blurted out. "What happened to me wasn't really scary, just weird and creepy. My mother and my therapist are making me come to this group. But I'm really okay." I could feel my face getting hot. What a dumb thing to say!

What Is Rape?

Rape is the forced act of sexual intercourse. In legal terms, rape is a type of sexual assault. It is committed by using threats, bullying, fear, and physical harm, or by using alcohol or drugs to get the person to go along with having sex, or to be less likely to fight back, even though she is no longer able to give legal consent. A person who rapes often uses force, either real or threatened. It can be committed by someone known to the victim or by a stranger. Rape is about power and control.

"How do you know what happened to me?"

"When you said that about being attacked in your bedroom, I thought maybe you were that girl in the newspaper."

"Oh." She was already small, but now she looked tiny, sort of shrunk in on herself.

"Being attacked by a stranger is the least common kind of child sexual abuse." Carol said. "Most sexual abusers are someone the child knows, often someone in the young person's family. Either way it can be disturbing and traumatic. That is where this group comes in. I can't undo the harmful things that happened to you, but I can try to help you get the

> **A Few Facts about Sexual Abuse**
>
> - Just less than half of all sexual abusers (30-47%) are related to the child they abuse.
> - Another half (49-50%) of all abusers know the child, but are not related.
> - About 40 percent of children are abused by older or larger children who they know.
> - Only about 4-10 percent of people who abuse children are strangers.[3]

information you need to make as much sense as you can about what happened. Talking and listening with your therapists and in this group will help you get to a place emotionally where you no longer feel so overwhelmed by sadness and fear. You will learn new ways to recognize dangerous situations and keep yourselves as safe as possible. You will learn to honor the ways that you have used to protect yourself, even as you are learning healthier ways to cope.

"I'd rather be abused by a stranger than someone living in my own home," Imaya said angrily, flicking her fingers as if she were trying to get dog slime off of them. Danielle flinched.

"I'll give you a handout about some of the reasons people respond differently to similar types of abuse," Carol said. "Each person is unique. Even if the same exact abuse happens to two kids at the same age, the feelings each of them have about it will be different." She paused and looked at each of us in turn.

"Now here is the most important thing, so please listen closely. I propose that in this group we try not to compare what happened to each of us as better or worse, or more or less hurtful. It's just not very helpful." I felt myself relaxing.

"My stepfather abused me," Imaya said in a tight, hard voice, as deep frown lines formed in the center of her forehead. "After my mother found out what he was doing to me, she left him. He kept trying to find us. We had to stay in the Women's Shelter for a while. He's in jail now." She crossed her hands over her chest and tucked her hands under her armpits.

"That sounds hard," Danielle said.

"I'm glad he is in jail. But now my mom is depressed and we can't afford anything."

Why Do People React Differently to the Same Type of Abuse?

There are lots of reasons why people react to abuse in particular ways. Some of these reasons include what was happening before and after the abuse, the type of support the person who was abused receives, and how that person feels about herself. Here are some other things that can impact the way a person responds to abuse.

- The age a person is at the time of the abuse.
- How old she is when she discloses or the abuse is discovered.
- How old she is at the time of the court hearings (if there are any).
- Whether the abuse happened one time, or over a long period of time.
- Whether she was abused by one person or more than one person.
- If she lost trust in someone she thought would protect her.
- If there was any violence or pain, or any threat of violence or pain.
- Who told about the abuse, how, and why.

continued ➻

- Whether she was believed, supported, and helped to feel safe and not at fault, or not believed, pushed aside, ignored, told to deal with the situation, or blamed for the abuse.
- If other family members experienced abuse when they were children.
- If her parents are physically abusive, neglectful, or violent toward each other, or if they have a problem with alcohol or drugs.
- If she feels like the "systems" meant to help her (child protection, police, courts, therapists, etc.) are helpful or hurtful.
- If the person who offended is very respected and well known in the community as a "good person," making a huge contrast with his or her secret abusive actions.
- If she lost a relationship with the person who offended because he went to jail or moved out of the home, or because she was moved out of the home.
- Where the abuse happened.
- If she believed the abuse was her fault.[4]

There sure are a lot of things that can go wrong, besides the sexual abuse. Abi

"That's not your fault," Danielle said. "He's the one who broke the law and screwed up your life."

"That's right," Carol said. "It is the abuser who is responsible for the sexual abuse, not the person who was abused. A lot of kids blame themselves when they have been abused. Next time in group we'll talk about why abuse happens, but right now I'd like to teach you a special way of breathing that can help you when you are feeling jumpy or nervous." Pictures from Phil's basement were going through my mind with the word "blame" blinking in neon pink letters in the background. I forced my attention back onto Carol. She was asking us to lean back and put one hand on our bellies and the other on our chests.

Chapter 6
. . . .
Breathing

"When we are anxious or upset we often start taking quick, shallow breaths, a pattern that tends to make us feel more panicky. Rapid breathing can even make you feel nauseated or dizzy. Slowing and controlling your breathing is a powerful way to calm yourself and help you feel in control of your body.

Try taking some slow, deep breaths through your nose right now. Bring the air all the way down so that the hand on your belly goes up when you breathe in. The hand on your chest should stay pretty still."

"We breathe like this in choir," I said. "Our choir director tells us to breathe *low.*"

Carol smiled, "Letting your belly go out gives your lungs more room to expand."

"I can't do it," Danielle said. Carol wanted her to lie down on the floor and shut her eyes to make it easier.

"If you think I am going lie down and shut my eyes —" Danielle shook her head.

"It makes me feel fat when I stick my belly out like that," Imaya said. Like anyone could think she looked fat!

"Abi and Imaya are getting it really well," Carol said. "Let's watch their hands move while I count. I want you all to really slow your breathing down, and relax as much as you're able." When everyone got the hang of that, Carol asked us to make each exhale take longer than the inhales.

"Choose a word that reminds you to relax and imagine saying it each time you breath out. Words like 'peace,' 'calm,' or 'mellow' work well."

Breathing

When people are upset it often shows in their breathing patterns. Instead of taking the slow, easy breaths your body needs, you might find yourself taking rapid shallow breaths, sucking in deep heaving sighs, or holding your breath. Changing how fast and how deeply you breathe changes the amount of carbon dioxide and oxygen in your blood. This can make your body feel strange. Rapid, shallow breathing can make you feel dizzy, nauseated, shaky, weak, or tingly. So ... if you are upset and you start to feel strange, remember to control your breathing. Nice and slow, in through your nose, out through your mouth is good. Relaxing your belly and letting it expand as you breath in will really help you calm down. You can also add a word to each breath that will help you to feel calm and safe. An example might be something like "hope," "calm," or "healing" with each exhale.

Sometimes lying on the floor can make it easier to feel your belly expanding. You might even want to put a lightweight book or a cup on your belly so you can see how the object moves when your belly moves. Let your chest stay relaxed and fairly still. This kind of breathing is sometimes called diaphragmatic breathing because it makes more room in your abdomen and pulls your diaphragm muscle down so your lungs have more room to expand.

"What about 'chocolate'?" Danielle asked. We all laughed. Maybe everyone was feeling like me — glad that Danielle seemed okay again. Carol looked at her watch.

"Great! We still have time to practice some listening skills." She had us divide up into groups of two. I was hoping I would get to be with Danielle, because at that point I was thinking I'd like to be friends with her, but Danielle turned toward Imaya. Jessica and Tara turned toward each other, so that left me with Carol. At least I didn't get stuck with Jessica.

"People need to be listened to." Carol said. "Just having someone listen carefully to what you are saying can be very comforting and healing. Sometimes it is hard to listen because we don't know what to say. So this exercise is about how to show you are listening without saying anything." It sounded stupid to me. "We will take turns being the listener and the talker. The talker will talk for five minutes about pleasant memories having to do with music. The listener is not allowed to talk, but she needs to show the talker she's interested. Then we will switch roles for another five minutes. Any questions?"

Getting Support

Feeling heard is a big deal. Getting all the attention you need from someone who cares about you and believes in you will help you heal from hard stuff. Telling safe people what happened to you can help you think about it with less trouble and move beyond feelings that can be overwhelming.

Healing doesn't happen in the same way or in the same amount of time for everyone. Be patient with yourself and learn to listen to and trust yourself. Find someone you trust to be with you while you express your feelings. It can help to be near someone. Having someone with you may help you to feel safer and allow you to experience strong emotions without feeling alone.

"What if we can't think of anything to say?" Danielle asked. "Just do your best," Carol answered. I told Carol I didn't mind talking first. I have lots of nice memories about music. It is about the one thing me and my mom and dad all do together. Ever since I can remember when we drive someplace we sing songs. We sing church songs and camp songs and Beatles songs and John Denver songs and some old Scottish Ballads my dad knows. I started talking about that and then I talked about how just last week I found out I was one of the three kids in our school choir selected to go to state honor choir. The whole time I was talking Carol really seemed to be listening even though she didn't say anything. She kept nodding her head, and smiling in the right places and sometimes opening her eyes up wide, like when I said I was selected for honor choir. I was just starting to explain what honor choir is when Carol's little timer started beeping. "Finish up quickly and switch," she said.

Carol talked about playing her cello. She showed how she holds it. I could almost see it nestled between her arms and legs. Sometimes when she practices, her dog, which was bred to be a sled dog but wasn't fast enough, starts howling along. She said he is very musical. I was listening to Carol and nodding. Out of the corner of my eyes I noticed everybody else seemed to be talking or listening right along, too, even Jessica and Tara. After the timer beeped, we all talked about what it felt like to be the listener and the talker and then it was time to go.

I went out to the waiting room. Right in front of the other girls in the group my mother announced we were going to be giving Jessica a ride home. I stopped myself before I groaned out loud.

After we let Jessica off my mother accused me of being impolite.

"But I didn't say anything!"

"Your silence was extremely rude. And when you frown and avoid looking at someone it sends a very unfriendly message. That is unacceptable, Abi. No matter how you feel about Jessica, I expect you to at least be courteous." She had her robot-mom look on her face. It seemed like nothing I did was right.

"You can't make me talk to her."

"Jessica is a very unhappy girl. She doesn't need your cruelty. If you can't be polite to Jessica, then you can't use the phone to call your friends." She was pulling in to my grandmother's house. Like *I wasn't* unhappy. Like I *had* any friends to call. All my real friends were back in California. We didn't even have a computer so I could chat with them. I wished we hadn't moved to Alaska. It was just so my mother could be closer to her mother. I liked my grandma but she could have moved to California if she needed help, instead of us moving to the end of the Earth.

Grandma said hello to me but I could tell by the way her smile iced up she was mad at me. Probably thought my skirt was too short. She doesn't like the way I dress. In her day the girls probably had to wear skirts to their ankles. I got out my homework and by the time I was done with my math, Mom had put the groceries away and finished

> ## The Importance of Anger
> Anger is important because it tells us that something is wrong, or that someone has hurt us.

helping Grandma go through her mail. Mom and I got into the car and I turned the radio to AM 105.3. They play the best songs with the least commercials. The sunshine made me happy and I sang along until we got home.

My dad came to the door. He kissed Mom and gave me a hug. After Mom went into the kitchen he asked me, "How's my Baby?" Unlike my mother, my father always asked how I was doing. I told him a little about school. Then I played piano for him like I usually did, while he relaxed.

After I went to bed I kept thinking about the group. I wondered why Tara was in the group. She seemed so normal. Actually everybody in the group seemed normal except Jessica. I had noticed Imaya at school before. She was in seventh grade, too, but she hung out with the jocks. I wondered what Carol was going to say about what causes sexual abuse. I was sure I had, at least partly, caused Phil to want to photograph me because I'm cute and friendly and because I sort of liked it.

As soon as I thought it, though, another part of me started arguing with myself. It was like listening to a whole room full of people in my own head. I couldn't think about that very much because my stomach started to hurt. I switched to playing piano in my head, trying to remember the pieces I was learning for my next piano recital. It still took me over an hour to fall asleep.

Underneath Anger

There are bigger, more tender emotions that hide under anger. Anger serves as a protection against having to deal with the uncomfortable feelings of loss, hurt, fear, loneliness, abandonment, and rejection. These "core" feelings are always under the anger though, and until you deal with the core hurts, you can't move on, and you can't "just forget about it."

I feel angry a lot. Abi

Reasons Kids May Think They Caused the Abuse

★ You may have wanted attention or love from the person who abused you. (Totally normal. We all want love and attention.)

★ Some of the touching may have felt good or exciting. (Many types of touching feel good. Our bodies are made to enjoy sexual touching.)

★ It may feel terrifying to accept that you did not have control over making the abuse happen. (Sometimes accepting reality is harder than believing that you could have stopped it.)

★ You didn't say "no" to the abuse. (Most people don't. Even if you had, the abuser probably wouldn't have listened.)

★ The person who abused you was your friend or a family member. (We often make excuses for people that we care about but this is also one of the things abusers use to keep you quiet.)

continued ➨

Reasons Kids May Think They Caused the Abuse (con't.)

⭐ You may have been abused when you were doing something you weren't supposed to be doing, like after you sneaked out of the house, or while you were at a party. (No matter what else you were doing, even if you were breaking family rules, you did not deserve to be abused. You did not cause the abuse to happen by anything you did, or said, or wore.)

⭐ You might not feel like you were abused at all. Maybe the sexual contact felt special to you and you can't figure out why all the adults around you keep saying that it was abuse (the law says that a child cannot make the decision to be sexual with an adult because the adult holds more power in the relationship.)

⭐ All of these responses to abuse are NORMAL. The child is not responsible for causing the abuse. The child did not control the abuser's behavior.

Chapter 7

. . . .

Why Does Sexual Abuse Happen?

"Thursday finally came. Unfortunately we were giving Jessica a ride both to and from group. From my vantage point inside the school I could see her out on the sidewalk in her own personal uniform of a huge flannel shirt and blue jeans. She never wore a coat. When I saw our red Blazer coming, I ran out past Jessica so I could get the front seat.

"Hi, Jessica," I said, for my mother's sake. Jessica whispered "Hi" from the back seat. My mother frowned at me. Why should I even try? I thought.

When Jessica and I got into the group room, everyone else was already there. I plopped down on the couch next to Imaya, who kind of shifted away from me. She seemed snobby. Jessica settled herself in the green bean bag chair like the week before.

Carol smiled at us kind of mischievously. She had a big cloth shopping bag, which she said had some things in it she had found around her house. Actually, she said the things had asked to be in the bag. Weird. We were supposed to pass the bag around the circle and reach in and pick out something our hand liked. There were a lot of different things in the bag, some sharp, some soft. My hand closed around a hard, interesting shape. I pulled out a white and gray rock with jagged edges. Imaya got a yo-yo and immediately started doing tricks with it. Her hands looked so dry they were kind of grayish. Tara cuddled a tiny teddy bear.

Jessica reached in quickly and grabbed a spruce cone. Then she shoved the bag to Danielle, who searched around for a long time and then pulled out a little metal train. Carol put her hand in, closed her eyes, took a deep breath, and pulled out a white glove.

We went around the circle and said how we were alike or different from what we had picked out. I was wondering what this had to do with the answer to why sexual abuse happens, which is what I'd been waiting to hear all week. Imaya said she was just like the yo-yo. Always moving, and sometimes she feels all wound up like the string around the yo-yo. I said I felt heavy like the stone, and I wished I could crash through a window into a different world. I was surprised to hear myself say that, but once I had said it, I knew it was true. I'd like to be in a simple world where I feel happy, and everybody likes me, and there is no such thing as sexual abuse.

I didn't say all that out loud.

> ## Wanting to Get Back at the Person Who Hurt You
>
> Sometimes people are so angry about their abuse or the abuse of someone they love that they focus on wanting to punish the offender. This can be important and healthy for a while, but if it goes on for a long time, or stops a parent from being able to focus on their child, it doesn't help with your healing process (and sometimes it even makes it harder!).

Danielle talked about feeling like she's on a train moving through a strange country she has never seen before. I nodded my head. I know that feeling. Jessica said she's like a spruce cone, because she doesn't say much. Then she gave that stupid little giggle she does with her hand over her mouth.

After pushing up her glasses, Tara said, "I'm more like a bear than a teddy bear." She's almost as short and small as Danielle so I didn't know what she was talking about. Carol asked her if she meant she feels powerful. Tara shook her head no. "More like wanting to hurt someone." She looked like she felt sick to her stomach.

Carol nodded a little at Tara and looked thoughtful. Then she looked down at the glove she was holding. "I'm more like a hand than a glove now. I used to be more like the glove." She said she feels surer about who she is and what she wants to do and she can be herself without trying to hide or be somebody else.

"Getting to know yourself is one purpose of this group," she said. "I want each of you to develop a stronger sense of what you love and what you hate and how you want people to treat you." She ran her fingers through her short hair. "Knowing who you are will help you heal from the sexual abuse, and also make it less likely you will be abused again." I wondered if Carol had been sexually abused and whether she had gone to a group like this. I wasn't sure I wanted to know who I really was, especially if I was the kind of person who was likely to be sexually abused.

"Let's talk a little about what sexual abuse is, and why it happens," Carol said. "Oh no," I thought, and, "Finally." It was weird feeling two opposite things at the same time. Carol picked up a magic marker and opened a big pad of paper on the easel next to her.

"What are some of the words that pop into your head when you think of defining sexual abuse," she asked us. Silence for at least a minute, then Danielle said, "Fear," in a scared little voice, and I quickly said, "It's illegal." I was hoping Danielle wasn't going to have another fit. Pretty soon everyone was saying things.

"Being tricked into doing something you don't want to do."

"Being forced to do something you don't like."

"Bad secrets"

"Ashamed"

"Alone"

"Getting touched by a creep"

"Child molesters"

"Pedophiles," Danielle said wrinkling her short nose.

"What is a pedophile?" I asked.

"Pedophiles are perverts. They like to have sex with children," Danielle said, sticking out her tongue like she was gagging. Talk about dramatic.

Carol nodded. "Some people who sexually abuse children are also attracted to adults. Pedophiles are primarily interested in being sexual with children." She put down the marker.

"Children may be tricked into trusting an abuser by his friendly behavior. He makes them feel as if they are his special friends." Carol linked her index fingers. "Gradually his behavior with them becomes more and more sexual. It can be very confusing. By the time kids figure out there is something weird going on, they may feel like it is too late to back out." She held her hands palm up and shrugged. "They often feel responsible for the abuse because there are many pleasant and enjoyable things about the relationship with the person who befriended them. The sexual abuse itself might have parts that are fun and exciting."

"Phil the Pedophile," Jessica muttered and covered her mouth. I started to laugh and then choked it back. I didn't want anyone to think I actually liked her. I still had the rock in my hand. I pressed the edge into my fingertips to make little rock shaped dents.

> **Myth: It happened because the person who abused was using alcohol or drugs.**
> **Fact:** This is a favorite excuse of offenders, but it isn't true. Offenders sometimes "set themselves up" by allowing themselves to use drugs or alcohol in order to excuse their sexual behaviors.[1] Even though there is often alcohol or drug use going on during the time of abuse, that doesn't mean that it caused the abuse. Many people drink and use drugs. Only a few people sexually abuse others. Abusers sometimes provide alcohol or drugs to their victims to make their victims more willing and less difficult to control.

Myth: It probably won't happen again.
Fact: It is unusual for an abuser to get caught the first time he or she abuses.[2] Most people who have abused once have abused other times, and some have abused several, even hundreds of other children. About 25 percent of abusers are themselves under the age of 18, and many abusers began abusing when they were youth.[3]

Scary!! Abi

"I don't think Eddie is a pedophile," Imaya said, her dark eyes thoughtful. "I don't know if he abused other kids besides me. He abused my mother, though. Not sexual abuse, I don't think, but he hurt her. A couple of times when he was on meth I thought he was going to kill her. I never trusted him, even when he wasn't using drugs. He scared me."

"Is Eddie your stepfather?" I asked. Imaya nodded, then shook her head.

"Was. My mom is divorcing him."

"Imaya has pointed out that sexual abuse isn't the only kind of abuse. What are other kinds of abuse?" Carol asked.

"Wife abuse."

"Child abuse."

"Cruelty to animals." That was Danielle. "Some people are really abusive to their pets. And sometimes scientists torture animals for the sake of stupid experiments."

"Well my cousin has to take insulin for his diabetes or else he'll die," Jessica said, "and insulin was only discovered by doing experiments on dogs. I don't think that was abuse. It was needed." She smiled and covered her mouth.

"It was abuse to the dogs," Danielle said, her cheeks turning pink. "Even if it was for a good cause, the scientists were using the dogs for their own selfish reasons. They weren't doing it for the dogs' sake." She shook her fist, making her hair jiggle. "The dogs were prisoners." I felt confused. I'd never thought about whether it was bad to use animals for experiments before.

After a pause Tara spoke up. "One time at a potlatch one of the Elders said that we should have respect for all living creatures. He said that cruelty to animals leads to cruelty to people."

Imaya got up suddenly and left the room saying she had to use the bathroom. Which was no big deal, except I realized that every single group she had to get up in the middle and go to the bathroom at least once. I wondered if she has diabetes. A boy I knew in California had to pee all the time until he found out it was because he needed to take insulin.

"Whether it is okay to use animals for experiments that will help people is a hard question. People have strong arguments on both sides of the issue," Carol said. "It may be that in the future animals will be given more rights and protections under our laws. Not too long ago, children and women were viewed almost like animals are now. According to the laws, a husband owned his wife and children. They had very few rights. It was even legal for a man to beat his wife, and for parents or teachers to beat children."

"That's assault."

"That's right, Abi. It's now illegal for anyone to beat a child or in fact for anyone to purposely physically injure another person in his or her household. When someone hurts or uses a less powerful person for his or her own selfish reasons, it is abuse. When sexual feelings are involved, it is called sexual abuse. The abuser is not considering the rights and feelings of the other person."

Danielle shivered. "When that man was abusing me, it was like I wasn't even a person to him. He treated me like a dog."

"Phil didn't treat me like a dog, he treated me nice," I said, and then wished I hadn't.

"He treated me nice, too," Jessica said. "He told me I had a wonderful mind. He said that ... he said that it is what is inside a person that makes them beautiful." Her face got puffier and she started crying. I felt embarrassed. Why had I opened my big mouth?

"Oh, Jessica, that's awful," Danielle said. "Do you think he was just trying to use you?" Jessica nodded.

"All that talk about my mind and he just wanted to touch my boobs."

> **Myth: People who abuse are "crazy."**
> **Fact:** Very few sex offenders suffer from a mental illness that causes them to be out of touch with reality.[4] Most people who abuse sexually are well aware of what they are doing, and usually plan out their abusive actions.

I laughed. Jessica's shoulders started shaking with her sobs. Danielle leaned over and put her arm around Jessica's back as far as she could reach. She scowled at me.

"You don't have to be abusive."

"It just sounded funny to me. I'm not abusive!"

Carol looked at me. "That's right, Abi, for something hurtful to actually be abuse, someone stronger or more powerful has to be trying to use or control someone less powerful. You and Jessica are equals. And sometimes we laugh when we feel embarrassed. But I do want this group to feel safe and supportive."

She took a deep breath and glanced at the clock on the wall. "Speaking of feeling safe, I'd like to take a little time for each of you to create your own safe place. Have any of you done this with your therapist?" Everyone must have looked as puzzled as I felt, because she kept explaining.

"A 'safe place' is a place you visualize where you can go if you are having scary or overwhelming emotions. It can be indoors or outdoors, a real place you remember, or an imaginary place. The important thing is that when you are there you know you are completely safe."

"I have a place like that, already," Imaya said quietly. "I thought there was something wrong with me because I go there a lot."

"Nope. It probably helps you stay sane," Carol said. Imaya didn't answer, but she gave her head a tiny little shake.

Carol asked us each to imagine going to a safe place. At first I started thinking about the bedroom where I stay when we visit my grandparents in California, but thinking about them made me feel sad, so I started making up an imaginary room in my mind that was sort of like that room, but I could put anything I wanted there. I moved in a piano, of course, and lots of pillows in all shades of green, for lounging around on. There were open windows that let in the sound of birds and the smell of flowers from the meadow outside. Inside, the walls were a pale rose color and the thick carpet under the pillows was a dark purple, the color of the center of some poppies I saw once in California.

When we talked afterward, I was surprised that I was the only one who had a room. Every single other person had safe places outdoors. Imaya talked about how she turns into a whale and swims with others of her kind in an underwater garden in the center of the ocean. Danielle invented a cave hidden behind a waterfall, guarded by three dragons. Tara had a secret outdoor place she liked to go to in real life, and she just pictured herself going there on a sunny day, with no mosquitoes. Jessica had a place on another planet. I could make a comment about that, but I won't.

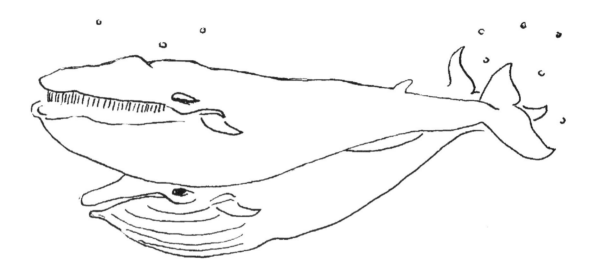

After that Carol wanted us to practice listening to each other again. I got Imaya. We talked about memories with animals. She had to give up her cat when she and her mom went to the women's shelter. I wanted to ask her more about that, but I could only try to show how sad I thought that was with my eyes, because we were still supposed to just listen. At the end of the group Carol gave us a handout of definitions. It wasn't until I was lying in bed that night that I realized Carol hadn't really said what makes sexual abuse happen.

Creating a Safe Place

A safe place is somewhere you can go to in your imagination when you are overwhelmed or scared, when you want to feel relaxed, or you can't go to sleep. You may have an actual "safe place" that you can go to, like your tree house, your friend's room, or the canoe you paddle on the lake. Or, it might be the dream of somewhere you hope to see someday: a warm sunny beach; a dark, quiet forest; or a rain storm on the desert. It can also be somewhere totally imaginative, like the purple fairy forest of your childhood imagination, or the deep blue of the ocean, swimming with a pod of whales.

Wherever your safe place is, think about all the sounds, all the smells, all the sights, all the things you can touch and taste, and burn them into your imagination. All of these will help to plant the picture firmly in your mind and help you to think of it quicker when you are feeling scared or down. Write a story or a poem about your safe place, or draw a picture of it. If you don't feel very artistic, make a collage out of pictures you cut or rip out of magazines. This will help you to think of your safe place more quickly when you need it.

Think about your safe place whenever you want to feel safe, secure, or calm.

I still use this. Abi

Chapter 8

. . . .

No, Really, I Need to Know, Why Does Abuse Happen?

I kept thinking about the group. Carol had said abusers start to do sexual things with children gradually. I remembered how I felt uncomfortable when Phil had started saying a few things about my breasts and my body that felt kind of weird. It was after I already liked him a lot. And he didn't get the skimpy clothes out right away, only after I had worn some other ones that were okay. What would he have wanted me to do if he hadn't gotten arrested, if Jessica hadn't told on him? I guess he was using me for his own selfish reasons. Maybe I didn't make it happen. But I didn't make it stop happening. Jessica did.

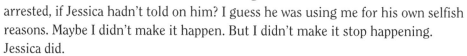

I tried to stay busy so I wouldn't think about it. I started playing piano again. I did my homework. I even helped clean out my grandmother's garage. At school, I started sitting with the kids that were friendly to me when I first moved to Bluff. Jake was there, too. I tried to ignore him. Amy and Shannon asked me if I wanted to go to a movie with them. I was glad people were treating me pretty normal, but

Was It Really Abuse?

Sometimes young people don't think what happened to them was abuse. Sometimes the people around them don't think what happened was abuse. When this occurs, a person may start to feel ashamed and lose trust in herself and in others.

I still worried about what they were thinking. I saw Imaya sitting at a table with some of the other kids that are good at sports. She wasn't talking much and then she got up before the bell rang and strode out by herself. She could be a model with her rich brown skin and high cheekbones and the way she walks with her hips forward and her shoulders back. I guess it's no wonder why she acts like a snob.

Thursday came. Carol had her big paper pad and easel again.

"You didn't tell us why sexual abuse happens." I couldn't keep myself from saying it right away. Carol gave me a quick smile that slipped away as she looked around at all of us. "It is hard to understand how something as hurtful as sexual abuse can happen. For many reasons, kids often think they did something to cause it. Kids don't cause child sexual abuse. It is the person who abuses who is responsible." Tara was sitting across from me silently shaking her head as if she disagreed. Carol didn't notice. She took the cover off of a magic marker. "Anybody have any ideas why someone might choose to sexually abuse another person?"

One True Reason

Most of the kids and the adults who were abused as children all have the same question: "Why me?" The problem with this question is that it is unanswerable. Even the person who abused you may not know why s/he chose you. There is only One True Reason. You were there. That's all. It may be that you happened to be there when the abuser was feeling needy, or hurt or shamed or angry. There is no specific thing that you did, said, or acted like that made the abuser become interested in you. Even if he has used this excuse to get you to feel badly, it isn't true!

I tattooed this handout onto my palm. Not really, but sometimes I wanted to. Abi

"Because they're jerks," Danielle said.

"Perverts!" Jessica blurted out.

"They can't get what they want from adults."
Danielle added. Carol just wrote the words down
without commenting

"I don't get it. I just don't get it. Sometimes
he was cool and fun to be with. He bought us
stuff. But then he ..." Imaya's voice cracked. Carol
put down her marker. She sighed.

"It's impossible to truly understand, but I can
tell you what I know. Some abusers are acting
out the angry or powerless feelings they have left over from being abused themselves.

"Well, I've been abused too, and I'm sure not going to do that to anyone." Imaya spit out her words. "Being abused
is no excuse."

"You are right, Imaya," Carol said, leaning toward her. Their brown eyes were locked together. "Reasons help
explain why someone might choose to act the way they do, but reasons don't make it okay. There is no excuse for
abuse. I'm talking about reasons with you because so many kids think they made the abuse happen. They didn't.
Anyone who has a problem that ends up hurting others has a responsibility to get help for that problem."

I felt like I was falling backwards into a deep hole. It still seemed like Phil wouldn't have abused me if I hadn't liked
all that attention.

> **Myth: People who offend sexually are themselves past victims of sexual abuse.**
> **Fact:** Most people who were abused do not abuse others. Some people who abuse others have been abused as children, but not all. Violent homes, where kids have witnessed abuse between parents, or were physically and/or emotionally abused themselves, and homes in which sex was too open or too secretive are also common childhood backgrounds of abusers.[1]

Body Image

Many people who have been sexually abused don't feel good about their bodies. Sometimes that's because of the kinds of things that the abuser said to them. If the abuser told you that you were beautiful, this might make you think (even though it's not true) that somehow you caused the abuse, or that it wouldn't have happened if you looked differently.

These types of messages make kids feel really confused. They may feel like their bodies betrayed them by responding to the sexual touching. They may feel dirty, or wonder if something is wrong with their bodies. They may not feel like they are really "in" their bodies. They may not feel safe in their bodies, or know where they end and someone else begins. They may use their bodies to get attention, or hide their bodies from everyone. They may feel uncomfortable in their bodies, or not know how to make them work right. They may stumble over themselves, and appear clumsy.

Sometimes these types of feelings can lead to eating disorders or hurting yourself. They can also lead to problems feeling comfortable with sex when you become an adult.

If you are having these types of feelings, it can help to do something physical. And it's a good idea to talk to a therapist about them.

Shame

Many people who have been abused feel shame. Even though you did nothing to make the abuse happen, a part of you may still feel ashamed about it. When a person feels shame they find ways to protect themselves from the feeling because it is such a strong and painful emotion. Most of the time we don't even realize that we're doing it. When a feeling of shame hits hard, automatic defenses kick in fast. Defenses are the things we use to protect ourselves from shame.

Defenses include things like pretending that the abuse didn't happen or that it wasn't that bad; telling yourself that it was your fault; making up excuses for the abuser's behavior; using drugs, alcohol, sex, or food to avoid feeling; becoming angry or aggressive, trying to be perfect at everything you do; hurting yourself; and trying to control others.

It may seem like these are negative behaviors, but that's not really the whole story. Defenses aren't meant to be harmful. They are meant to be a way of protecting the self from painful feelings. And people who have been sexually abused often learn to protect themselves from feelings of shame, fear or distress, even when it means hurting themselves in other ways.[2]

I hate that awful, sick-to-your-stomach, ashamed feeling. Abi

"What if there was, for example, a situation where the kid didn't think it was that bad?" I whispered.

"Yuck," Danielle said, sticking out her tongue like she was going to puke. I could feel my face getting hot. I felt sick.

"It is still the abuser's fault," Carol said. "Sexual feelings are supposed to feel good. Your body is made to enjoy those tingly, exciting feelings in your genitals, your private parts. It's just that it isn't fair for adults to be sexual with kids, or for anyone to force sexual activity on someone else. Kids don't cause sexual abuse by enjoying sexual feelings. It is normal to enjoy sexual feelings."

She kept talking but I couldn't hear what she was saying. My head hurt and I felt like I was going to throw up. I couldn't believe I had said that about a kid not thinking it was that bad out loud. I was too embarrassed to look at anyone. Carol put her hand on my arm.

"What is going on, Abi?" I shook my head. "You look really uncomfortable. I'd like you to take a slow deep breath into your belly." I took a deep breath. "Okay everyone, let's practice controlling our breathing. It helps with feelings. Breathe in through your nose — let your belly expand. Let your breath out slowly, making a hissing noise." We hissed slowly in unison. I laughed to myself, thinking of how we all sounded like upset cats, but my headache started to go away, so I guess it was worth it.

"It was that way for me at first," Tara said quietly. "At first I didn't think it was that bad. My brother and I were just kind of playing. I wanted him to like being with me. Then he started trying to get me to do stuff I didn't really want to do. I was so confused. It felt like we were in it together by then." Tara shook her head as if to shake the memories off. Her black hair flew out, then settled in curves at her neck. Her glasses slipped down her nose when she looked down. "After a while I started to hate my body for how it felt. I didn't want to feel anything. I didn't know how to get him to stop. He said I wanted it, too, and if I told Mom we'd both get in trouble."

"It is pretty common for children to explore their bodies with each other, especially brothers and sisters. If the kids are close to the same age and there isn't any pressure, it isn't sexual abuse. If there is a large age difference, if a bigger child is pressuring a smaller one to participate, or if several children are ganging up on another, that's different," Carol said. "It must have been confusing for it to go from being play to being abuse."

"If only I hadn't liked it at first maybe it never would have happened," Tara almost whispered.

"He still shouldn't have pressured you." Imaya sat tense and motionless, but her words were ragged and harsh.

I couldn't bear the silence that followed, with the pain from her words still hanging in the air.

"He sounds mean," I said to Tara.

"No, he's not. I mean, not usually. He's my favorite brother." She looked confused and shook her head. "Used to be, I mean. I don't know why he did that to me." Her voice started shaking, "I hate my body for feeling that way when he touched me."

"Our bodies respond if our sexual parts are touched. That's how the nerves are hooked up. If someone steps on your toe when you don't want him or her to, it hurts anyway. If someone holds a rose underneath your nose and you feel all mixed up about him or her doing that, it still smells like a rose. Your body can't help it." Carol stood up. "Let's get up and move our bodies."

The Difference Between Sexual Play and Sexual Abuse

Many children experiment with each other in a sexual way. Often siblings or friends will explore together. That type of sexual behavior is not abuse. There are important differences between normal (natural) sex play and sexual abuse.

Sex play: ✱

- Is about curiosity.
- Includes giggling or laughter.
- Occurs naturally, rather than being planned.
- Sometimes includes embarrassment, but not shame.
- Happens between children of similar age, size and status.
- Can involve kissing, touching, and looking.

Sexual Abuse:

- Happens in secret and isolation.
- Involves power, tricks, bargaining, making you feel scared or unsure of yourself.
- May include threats, or force.

continued ➣

The Difference Between Sexual Play and Sexual Abuse

Sexual Abuse (con't):

- The person being abused feels fearful and anxious, not giggly.
- There are big differences between the people involved in age, size, or power status.
- The kissing, touching or looking happens in a way that can change, or increase over time, moving into pushier and more personal acts.[3]

★ *It's nice to know that the stuff I did with my friends when I was little was normal. After that whole thing with Phil, I wasn't sure. Abi*

She had us push the couches and beanbags against the walls so there was more room in the middle. Then we played a game where we all had big fluffy imaginary space suits on. We had to show each other how thick our space suits were and we could make them as thick as we wanted. She put on some conga music and we danced around the room. No one could touch anyone else because of the space suits. It was kind of silly, but it made me feel better. Imaya smiled, Danielle giggled, Tara laughed, and even Jessica got into it.

Telling Without Words

Children often try to let adults know when something is wrong. Sometimes they do this by talking about it, but other times the words are just too hard to say, or the child doesn't know how or what to say. Sometimes what happened is bigger than words can express. So, they do other stuff to get the attention of grownups and to get their point across. Below are some of the ways that kids try to tell grownups that something sexual has happened to them without actually saying it out loud.

- Talking about abuse in general terms.
- Acting or playing with toys in a sexual way.
- Drawing pictures of genitals or breasts.
- Sudden or major changes in behavior.
- Eating more or less than usual.
- Sleeping problems.
- Stomach aches, headaches or other body pains.
- Wetting the bed.
- Acting younger.
- Acting older.
- Running away from home.
- Difficulty concentrating in school.
- Dropping grades.
- Using alcohol or drugs.
- Angry or aggressive behaviors.
- Staying away from a certain place or person, or from a certain type of person.

There are many different ways that kids try to tell, but they all have to do with a change in the way they used to act before the abuse. Sometimes kids and adults feel ashamed about the way that they acted after being abused, but it's important to see the good in the behaviors that you used to try to tell someone about the abuse. Even if they are no longer useful now, these behaviors once protected you from having to deal with feelings you weren't yet ready to deal with.

Chapter 9

Boundaries

The next day Imaya wasn't in school. People were saying she'd been sent to a mental hospital. I couldn't believe it. She looked so normal. Amy said the only weird thing she ever noticed about Imaya was that she was always washing her hands. Like twenty times a day. I guess that's why she always had to go to the bathroom. That didn't seem weird enough to get sent to a funny farm. I told my dad about it and he wasn't very nice. He said he wasn't sure he wanted me in a group with any nutso kids.

"Oh, Dad," I laughed, "You're such a worrier. Imaya is nice." I gave him a kiss on the cheek. He smiled and gave me a little pat on the bottom. "You're my girl, Abi, I don't want anything happening to you." He had been patting me on the bottom like that all my life. I never used to think anything about it, but lately I'd been wondering if the other girls would think it was weird. I thought I might ask my therapist, Jean.

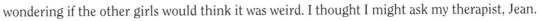
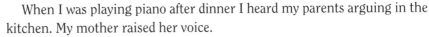

When I was playing piano after dinner I heard my parents arguing in the kitchen. My mother raised her voice.

"She will stay in the group, Bill." I heard the back door slam and my dad's footsteps on the porch. I get along better with my dad than my mother does.

In the group on Thursday everyone was talking about Imaya. We wanted Carol to tell us why she was in the hospital.

The Importance of Honoring How You Survived

Whatever you did to get through the abuse, those behaviors were important in letting others know how much you were hurting. They might also have helped you to survive your feelings about the abuse, which could have been more overwhelming without the acting out behaviors to distract you.

It is weird to think that back when I was so worried about the trial and flunking seventh grade, I might have been actually doing something positive — at least trying to let my parents know I needed some help with all my confused feelings. Abi

"That information belongs to Imaya. Let's wait and see how much she wants to share after she gets back," Carol said. "Sometimes kids who have been sexually abused have such strong and confusing feelings that they act in ways that can hurt themselves or others. In a hospital they get support for their feelings and help in controlling their behavior." Help in controlling their behavior sounded like something my mother would say before she sent me to my room, or grounded me for months.

"I wish I could write her a letter," Danielle said, "just to tell her I miss her in the group."

"Me too," I said. Carol promised to check on it.

She passed the river rock around and we talked about how we were doing and how our week had gone. I wanted to talk about my parents fighting, but I didn't. I told about a boy in school that I thought liked me. He kept looking at me during math. Carol wanted us to talk about boundaries and limits. If you have strong boundaries it means you don't get your feelings mixed up with other people's feelings. You don't feel like you have to try to keep other people from feeling bad. You tell someone to stop if they are doing something you don't like. I was thinking that my boundaries were somewhere deep inside of me instead of on the outside like they were supposed to be. Back then I couldn't really tell what were my real feelings and what were the feelings I was showing people so I wouldn't get hurt. My real feelings were inside down deep and sometimes I didn't even know what they were. On the surface, outside of my inner boundary, were the feelings I let other people see. I was getting confused just thinking about it. I started thinking about how I'd made such a horrible mistake with Phil. I should have had limits. But I wanted him to like me. He made me feel like I was special. And I didn't think what he was doing was that bad.

"So how do you know if a boyfriend, or anyone really, is respecting your boundaries?" Carol asked. I sat up straighter. I didn't want anyone to notice I wasn't listening. Everybody was looking at Carol, except Jessica. When she saw me looking at her she looked away. Her hair swung in greasy strings when she turned.

"They listen to you," Danielle was saying. "They care about what you are thinking and feeling."

"Yeah, and if you say no, they don't pressure you," Tara added. She flushed a deep maroon. "They aren't always pinching your breasts or patting your butt when no one is looking." I figured she must have been talking about her brother. But some of the guys I hung out with in California did that. It was kind of a joke. Once an older boy that I thought was cute pushed me up against the wall in a shopping mall and felt my breasts through my top. And

Sexual Touching, Love, and Respect

It is helpful if you don't use sexual touching to try to help yourself feel loved or desired until you feel healed from the abusive touching. If you use sexual touching as a way to get your needs met before you have healed, difficult memories and feelings can be set off and this can lead to confusion, anger and fear.

Be gentle with yourself, and stick up for your needs. Everybody has their own timeline for sexuality. What is right for one person may be wrong for another. If you have been sexually abused, it is particularly important to notice where your comfort level is and to honor it.

my father had patted my butt just last night. My stomach hurt.

"Are you saying if a guy pinches a girl's breasts or pats her butt it's sexual abuse?" I asked. Tara looked upset, but I had to know. Danielle put her hand on Tara's. I felt like I was the outsider.

"It's sexual abuse if the girl doesn't want him too!" Danielle said. Carol was looking at me. I made myself smile so she wouldn't start having me do that bizarre breathing thing. She took a deep breath and let it out. Maybe she was upset.

"Let's go slow with this," she said. "It's not an easy topic and we all have some strong feelings about it. I will let you know what I think and then I want your comments. Remember, we are in a safe place and we can explore some hard things. Talking about sexual touching in this group may feel scary, but it isn't dangerous." She took another deep breath and let it out slowly while she looked around at us with her warm brown eyes. I took a deep breath, too. It was kind of contagious. "Talking about it doesn't mean that I am encouraging you to do sexual things. You may not want to be sexual for years. But talking and thinking about what you want will help you be better able to keep yourself safe." She smiled reassuringly. "Okay?" We nodded.

"Say a guy is pinching a girl's breasts, or patting her bottom and she doesn't want him too, and she tells him so, and he keeps doing it. That would be sexual abuse, or when both are about the same age, it is usually called sexual harassment. But if you have a guy who is gently pinching his girlfriend's breast or patting her bottom when they are alone together, and she likes it, then it is not sexual abuse or harassment. That kind of attention can feel fun and exciting if both people want it. What is right for one person can be scary or harmful for someone else. Take things very slowly and notice what feels comfortable to you and the person you are with."

She reached into her bag and pulled out a big paintbrush. "Sexual touching is like this paintbrush."

"A paintbrush?" Danielle said. "What do you mean?"

The Difference Between Sexual Play and Sexual Harassment

Many children experiment with their budding sexuality and sexual feelings in a playful manner. That type of sexual behavior is usually not abuse. Sometimes, though, when the behavior becomes too aggressive, it can cross a line into sexual harassment. There are important differences between playful behaviors and sexual harassment.

Playful Behaviors:

- Are comfortable for everyone involved or witnessing the behavior.

- Often include giggling or laughter.

- Occur naturally, rather than being planned.

- Sometimes include embarrassment, but not shame.

Sexual Harassment:

- The behavior of the person doing the harassing is not welcomed by the person who feels victimized.

- Can include sexual behaviors, such as kissing, grabbing, pinching, pulling someone's shirt up, or their pants down; requests for sexual favors or acts; or comments about sex, sexual orientation or preference, or the person's sexual habits (for example, calling someone a "slut").

- The victim is not only the person who is the target of the harassment, but can also be anyone present who was negatively affected by the behaviors of the person doing the harassing.

- May include some of the same activities as the playful behaviors, but the other person or people involved do not like or want the behaviors to occur.[1]

Carol started painting in the air. "With practice, a person can learn to paint beautiful pictures with this, pictures that come from deep within, and that are as individual as the person painting them. One person might paint quiet landscapes, another dramatic colors and shapes, and someone else, a different kind of painting every week. There are lots of different ways to be sexual."

"Sexual touching isn't beautiful if you don't want it!" Danielle crossed her arms and frowned.

Carol put the brush down. "Sexual abuse is like using the paintbrush to hit someone, instead of for painting." She looked around the room at each of us. "Now, what are your reactions to what I just said?" Nobody said anything. I was thinking about my dad and wondering if he had touched me sexually when he patted my bottom. My dad had never touched my breasts, but Carol kept putting that together with butt-patting like it was the same thing. I was afraid to say anything. What if it turned out my father was a sex abuser for patting my butt and he got put in jail? He kissed me on the lips, too. Maybe that was illegal. I didn't know the stuff with Phil was illegal. It didn't seem like my dad was trying to hurt me when he patted my butt. Phil wasn't trying to hurt me either. At least I didn't think so. Or maybe he was.

Defining Your Boundaries

If you are a heterosexual girl ask yourself: Am I able to have nonsexual friendships with boys?
If you are a lesbian ask yourself: Am I able to have nonsexual friendships with girls?
If you are bisexual or unsure about your sexual orientation ask yourself both questions.

Testing out your comfort level by talking with friends of both sexes about all kinds of things, including your boundaries, will help you to feel more clear about who you are.

"So if you ask a guy to stop and he doesn't that's what makes it sexual harassment?" Danielle asked.

"Yes," Carol said. "Both people have to want to participate. If both people care about each other and respect each other's values, sexual touching can be okay. It's complicated, though, especially when someone has been hurt by sexual touching. I recommend you girls take things slowly. Give yourself time to untangle your normal, healthy sexuality from the sexual abuse. It may take a number of years before you are ready to try sexual touching. And you may want to wait until you are in the safety of a marriage. Some people believe that is the best way."

I couldn't keep my mouth shut. "It isn't that big of a deal for the kids in California. I know at least three girls that aren't virgins anymore. They really aren't virgins." I just kept blundering on. "And it is kind of a joke if a guy pinches a girl's breast or something. And the girls do it, too, not pinching breasts of course, but patting a guy's butt or making a comment about his buns. It's not abnormal or anything."

"Some girls are just sluts," Danielle said, looking disgusted.

Jessica looked at her hands. Tara had a blank look on her face. Obviously, Danielle was talking about me. I hoped my dad would make me drop out of the group. I could see that Carol's lips were moving again and she was leaning forward the way she does when she's explaining something she thinks is important. Her words weren't making any sense to me.

What Kind of Relationship Do You Want to Be in Before You Participate in Sexual Touching?

Do you want to be in a long-term, loving, committed relationship? Married? Dating? How will you know when you feel ready to participate in different kinds of touching? How will you react if someone tries to push your boundaries?

What Are Your Parents' Values and Beliefs about Sexual Touching?

Do you agree with them? Are you willing to go by their rules or guidelines? If not, what are your rules and guidelines about sexual touching?

Personal Space

Some people are very aware of their personal space boundaries and they are able to tell others what those boundaries are. Other people are not aware at all of where they end and another person begins. Some people have large personal space boundaries and they are uncomfortable when another person is in their body space. Other people don't mind or even notice when someone gets very close to them.

"A lot of girls dress to get attention." Danielle said. "They want guys looking at them and thinking about them that way. I think it's gross. I'm not saying they deserve to get raped or anything, but…"

"Yeah, right! That is exactly what you are saying," I blurted. My mouth … I wished I had duct taped it before I came to the stupid group.

Carol smiled at us. "This is great stuff to talk about. There is so much confusion about it. So, what do you think? Say a girl wears a skimpy top and a short skirt and is very flirtatious. If she gets raped, is it her fault?" Tara and Jessica were shaking their heads, no, but Danielle rolled her eyes.

"I know what you want us to say, that it's the guy's fault, but I still think she is asking for it in a way."

"Okay," Carol said, "do you think an elderly man wearing an expensive suit and walking through an area with a lot of bars,

What are Your Values and Beliefs about Sexual Touching?

How old do you think people should be before they kiss, French kiss, touch another person's genitals or breasts, do oral sex, have sexual intercourse? How long should you know someone before you kiss or touch intimately? Do you think people should be married before having sex? Why or why not? What about gay people who can't legally marry in most states? If you are being pressured to be more or less sexual than you feel good and confident about, consider talking to a therapist or trusted adult about your feelings.

It's embarrassing to think about this stuff — but you can do it. Abi

Practice Stepping Away

One simple way to ask for more space is to just step away from someone who is too close. If you have a friend or family member whom you trust to work with you, you can practice stepping away or saying no.

alone, late at night, is asking to be robbed?"

"That would be stupid," Danielle said.

"Maybe the girl isn't asking to be raped, maybe she is just asking for someone to notice her and she doesn't think it will turn out the way it does." Jessica whispered.

"Could be," Carol nodded, "or maybe she is terrified that people will approach her sexually and she wants to get it over with — to feel like she is more in control of it." We must have looked confused because she went on. "When a person has been hurt sexually, she or he often goes to one extreme or the other. Some people try to avoid anything remotely having to do with sex. On the other end of the spectrum are those who act overly sexual. They may dress and act in ways that seem to broadcast that they are available for sex. It may not look like it, but both extremes are born from fear and confusion."

Sexual Abuse and Personal Space

Sexual abuse can mess up the way a person thinks about personal space. Sometimes sexual abuse makes a person feel like they need lots and lots of room between themselves and others, and sometimes sexual abuse makes a person think that it's okay for anyone to get as close as they want, even when they don't want the closeness themselves. Some people don't even know that they have the right to tell others what their personal space limits are. Many people know they have the right, but do not know how to say what their limits are.

Whatever ... It's all Good ... It doesn't Matter ...

Learning to value yourself is another important step to becoming assertive. When you were sexually abused you were taught that your body and your feelings did not matter. Such interactions can cause a person to believe that they don't have the right to want or need anything. You matter, and you have a right to your own thoughts, feelings, and opinions. If you are having trouble believing this, talking to a therapist may help.

Danielle shook her head, jiggling her curls. "I still don't get it. But I guess I'll try not to be so quick to judge girls I think are acting like sluts." There was a long pause, and then Tara said, "I'm sick of that word."

Danielle looked surprised. "Oh. Sorry."

Carol took a deep breath and then said slowly and clearly, "No matter what a person wears or how a person acts, it never gives anyone the right to force sex on them." I wouldn't have minded if she had repeated that four or five times, but I didn't say anything.

"The thing is," Carol said, "people who have been sexually abused may be confused about what normal, respectful behavior looks like. They may be unsure about whether or not someone is touching them or speaking to them inappropriately. This can increase their risk of being abused again. I want to help each of you get clear about your personal boundaries." I wondered if she thought all of the kids I used to hang out with in California were sexual abuse victims or abusers.

"Let's make a list of signs someone is respecting your boundaries and signs someone isn't," Carol said. I didn't say much. I figured I'd already put my foot in my mouth enough times for one day.

Late that night I wrote to Imaya. I wondered what she was doing. I wondered if she would have felt as left out as me during the group, or if she would have been just one more person against me.

Dear Imaya,

I'm sorry you had to go to the Hospital. I hope it is okay there. Is it nice, or is it awful? I really miss having you in the group. We talked about boundaries and guys touching girls' boobs or butts today. It made me upset. Everyone misses you in the group. Maybe we can do something together when you get back. I hope you get well soon. Please write back.

Your friend (I hope),

Abi

Chapter 10

. . . .

Forgiveness (Not!)

At church that Sunday I saw Jessica sitting with Margaret Andersen and her girls. She's the woman whose husband drowned when his fishing boat went down. My mom told me Mrs. Andersen couldn't put the littlest girl in the nursery during church because ever since her daddy died she totally loses it if her mom leaves her even for an instant. The older girl was sitting in Jessica's lap. Jessica's parents were sitting in church, too, but further toward the back.

The gospel reading was about when someone asked Jesus how many times you should forgive someone who hurts you and he said seventy times seven. The pastor, George Powell, talked about forgiveness during his sermon. He told a story about two brothers who didn't talk to each other for years. Hatred connects people in rigid, hard ways, the pastor said. Forgiveness and love loosen the old connections and let people bend and change. It's like people can be connected in a different way.

By the end of the sermon I was feeling kind of sick. First there was Jessica. I didn't really hate Jessica as much anymore, but I was afraid people would lump us together if I wasn't mean to her. Besides, I wasn't sure what exactly she had done to me that I might need to forgive. I didn't want to be connected to Phil, either. I never told anybody this, but sometimes I missed him. I had to hate him so I wouldn't wish I could see him again. So what! if God had a problem with that? I had to stay hating Phil. My head was aching.

During coffee hour Dad came up to me and said Pastor Powell wanted to talk to our family afterward. I asked him why but he said he didn't know. When we got to the church office, who should be there already, but Jessica and her parents. She's like a recurring nightmare.

Forgiveness

Forgiveness means that you want to be free from the shame and pain and anger that you have been holding, and you choose to give it back to the person it belongs to — the person who abused you. It means that you are ready to be whole again, that you are allowing yourself to see your potential and your goodness. You free yourself from the ties that have bound you to the person who abused you. It means that you let go of the hate and anger that has stopped you from being able to connect with yourself and with other people. It means that you forgive the core self of the person who hurt you, but you are not accepting or excusing the behavior of that person. Forgiveness is really for you, not for your abuser. Forgiving does not mean forgetting; you may never be able to trust the person who abused you. Your relationship with that person will never be the same as it was before the abuse. And forgiving does not excuse the abuser from fulfilling any promises or conditions of parole or probation or treatment.

I still don't really get it. Abi

Mr. Powell smiled in his kindly way. "While I was giving the sermon on forgiveness today, I looked out and saw you girls." He looked first at Jessica and then at me. I could feel my face getting hot. "I started worrying maybe it wasn't quite the right sermon for you two. Phil abused you. You were betrayed by your church, including me, since we were the ones who hired Phil to be the youth leader. It would be very natural for you to feel angry toward Phil, and toward our church and me." He scratched his ear. "Indeed, it is healthy for a person to feel angry after they have been tricked or hurt by another person." He seemed to be moving into sermon mode, but I was listening.

"Forgiveness is not something to rush into if you have a lot of raw pain and anger about being abused," Pastor Powell went on. "Those feelings can protect your wholeness and take you toward being a healthy adult. The important person to forgive is yourself. I'm not saying either of you caused the abuse. What happened with Phil was not you girls' fault. But if you are blaming yourselves for trusting him, or for keeping his secrets, you need to forgive yourselves."

I glanced over at Mr. and Mrs. Cornfield. They were both scowling and looking at a place just above the pastor's head. Jessica was looking down at the floor. It was so different from my parents who were looking at Mr. Powell and then looking at me and nodding with what he said.

"That's right, girls," my dad said. "It was that damned Phil's fault." Then he looked toward the pastor and clenched his jaws. "I don't think I'll ever be ready to forgive that, that," he paused. I knew he was trying to find a word that was okay to say in front of the minister and the Cornfields. "…That bastard," he finally blurted.

When Forgiveness Is Demanded

Family members, community elders, or religious leaders may insist or demand that you forgive the person who abused you. You may feel that you have to comply to keep peace in your community or family. Some Christian churches require that their members forgive any people who have harmed them. But in the Christian scriptures, there's no specific time line for that to happen. Take your time so that when you do forgive, it can be a genuine forgiveness, even if that seems to take forever. And remember, forgiving the person does not mean accepting or excusing the behavior, and it doesn't mean forgetting what happened or trusting the abuser again.

Forgiving Doesn't Mean Forgetting

Forgiving someone does not mean forgetting the abuse! Forgiving doesn't mean that you don't want to see the offender get some kind of consequence for the hurt he or she caused you. It doesn't mean that you can or are going to trust him again, or that you would want to be in the same room with him. It doesn't mean that you don't have big feelings about the abuse or the abuser. If the abuser denies that it happened or blames you for the abuse, it will be harder, or even impossible, to forgive. Forgiveness can be complete, partial, or not at all. The choice to forgive should be yours.

Forgiving Yourself

Forgiving yourself might be an important step to healing. Many people who have been abused blame themselves for the abuse. Remember that a child or teenager is never to blame for sexual attention from an adult. If you feel like the abuse was your fault, it might be useful to talk to a therapist or to another survivor of sexual abuse. If you can't do that, imagine someone you know as a victim of sexual abuse. Would you blame that person for being abused? If not, then you might rethink how you are treating yourself.

Pastor Powell looked at my father in a nice way, not smiling but with warm eyes. He took a big breath and let it out the way Carol sometimes does. "We need to let our hearts lead us, Bill. God is big enough for our anger."

My mother sat up straighter, and leaned away from Dad. "I blame myself for what happened." That was news to me.

Mr. and Mrs. Cornfield glanced at each other.

"Phil just isn't the kind of guy that would do something like that," Mr. Cornfield blurted gruffly. "We think this is a bunch of baloney that the girls dreamed up at school."

If You Are Not Believed

When sexual abuse happens in a family, or when the abuser is a family friend or a respected member of the community, some people in the victim's family or community may find it hard to believe. If this is happening to you, and especially if you are being blamed for the abuse, it is much harder to heal (but not impossible!). Talk to a therapist about how to deal with this.

My mind was going bonkers. This did not compute. I mean, Phil was already in jail, for one thing, and for another thing, Jessica and I never talked to each other at school. From the looks on my parents and Mr. Powell's faces, their minds were having trouble processing, too. Jessica was still staring at the floor. The parts of her face that I could see through her hair had turned bright red.

Mrs. Cornfield looked at her watch. "I hope you will excuse us, George. We need to get going to Carrie's swim meet. We can't miss her in the backstroke. She may pull off another new record." Jessica's little sister, Carrie, was one of the most popular girls in fifth grade.

Mr. Powell sighed. He gave Jessica a card. "Here's my phone number. Call me if you have questions or would like to talk." After the Cornfields left he shook his head as if to try to get things straightened out inside. He turned toward my mother. "I blame myself, too, Lois. Phil was so personable. I can see how Jessica's parents might have a difficult time believing that someone with so many good qualities could do something so hurtful. His references were good and he seemed to work well with the young people. I trusted him too much." He rubbed his forehead as if it hurt. "He was my friend." Inside my head I could hear my voice shouting, He was my friend, too. I didn't say anything.

My dad frowned. "That jerk sure pulled the wool over our eyes."

Before we left the pastor reminded us not to rush into forgiveness. "It takes time to heal. Your anger is healthy. Don't let anyone push you to forgive before you are ready." He gave us all cards with his phone number.

Chapter 11

The Fight

On Wednesday I spent an hour in after-school detention with Danielle. (This is an embarrassing story.) She'd come up to me in the hallway at lunchtime the day before and said she hated the way I'd been treating Jessica. She acted like Jessica was some poor helpless wild animal that she, Warrior Princess of the Society for the Prevention of Cruelty to Animals, needed to defend.

"We're in a support group together. We are supposed to be supporting each other," she hissed, Medusa-like with her snake hair. "Poor Jessica, she doesn't dare open her mouth with you around."

"Poor Jessica!" I said, trying to whisper, "What about me? I didn't ask to be in that stupid group with her."

"It isn't her fault you got abused by the same guy. You act like she was the one who abused you, not him." I slapped her. She grabbed my wrists and pushed me against the lockers. She was surprisingly strong for being so small. Mrs. Fortune, the principal, came up behind her and told us to come with her. She wanted to know why we were fighting. Danielle just sat there looking irate, both her cheeks bright red, not just the one I had slapped. Finally I said we were fighting about a boy we both liked. Danielle gave a short nod. Mrs. Fortune went on and on about how we were "role models for the students in the younger grades," assigned us detention, and said she would be notifying our parents.

When I got home my mother gave me another lecture. Then she said I could do some extra chores to help me remember not to fight in school. My dad talked to me when he got home, too. But he was mostly interested in who the boy was Danielle and I were supposedly fighting over. I didn't know what to say so I said it was Jake.

Anger Is Normal

Most people who have been sexually abused go through a period of being very angry. Even though the anger may feel out of control, it is a normal stage to go through. It is only a problem when you don't move through it into the harder, deeper work of what's under the anger, or if you hurt yourself or someone else when you are angry.

My dad said he thought I wasn't interested in Jake anymore.

"I bet all the junior high boys are secretly in love with you, Honey. You shouldn't worry about one guy." That made me laugh. He gave me a hug and asked me to rub his neck, because he had had a tough day at work. Sometimes it seems like my dad wishes he were my boyfriend.

When my mom picked Jessica and me up for group on Thursday, I noticed Jessica had washed her hair. It was actually fluffy and blond looking without all that grease.

"I won't need a ride home after group today," Jessica told my mom. "I'm staying with Margaret Anderson, and her house is just down the street from the Women's Resource Center."

"Yes. Your mother told me, Jessica." My mom turned on her warmest smile. "How wonderful you are helping Margaret. I feel so sad for her."

"Pastor Powell arranged it." Jessica said. I figured she was glad to be away from her own family. I was starting to wonder if how they treated her was emotional abuse.

Chapter 12

Feeling Mixed Up

Imaya still wasn't back in the group. I was glad I had brought my letter. When Carol said she could forward our letters to Imaya at the hospital, I was the only one who had one right then. Carol had her river rock again and she said she wanted us to have a talking circle about things we did in the past week we felt good about. She said people usually feel uncomfortable about bragging, but in a support group like ours, it was okay.

She went first, and said she felt good about speaking up when she had a different opinion from a friend about something important to her. It surprised me that Carol would have a hard time speaking up about something. She seemed so confident when she talked. Danielle said she was glad she had spoken up and told someone to stop being cruel to someone else. She seemed to think she was some kind of hero or something for picking that fight with me. Jessica got all glowy looking talking about how she rocked Margaret's little baby to sleep. It was the most I had ever heard her say. Tara said she had talked her mother into letting her have a puppy.

Suddenly it was my turn. I thought about saying I felt good about slapping someone, but that wasn't really true, and besides, I didn't want everyone to start asking questions. I didn't enjoy feeling despised by everyone in the world. I couldn't think of anything I felt good about.

How Do I Heal?

Some people will tell you that you have to talk about the sexual abuse in order to heal. You might think that this isn't true for you. Sometimes there are no words for what happened. Or the words are too powerful to speak. Sometimes abuse happens before a person has even developed language, and so there never were any words, only feelings related to what was experienced. But dealing with the abuse in some way is the only way to get beyond it.

Some people process the abuse by writing about what happened to them. Others sing, shake, rock, run, scream, dance, sweat, draw, write, sculpt, hike, or play. Sometimes people talk about the abuse but use code words.

Everyone was looking at me. I didn't want Danielle to know I couldn't think of anything. I guess I started panicking.

"Can anyone help Abi?" Carol asked. I glanced at Danielle sitting in the corner beanbag chair. I expected her to be gloating about how I was feeling so crummy, but she didn't seem to be that way at all. She was looking at me. Not mean, not triumphant, just sort of looking at me like she was seeing me. Maybe even seeing some inside part of me. I looked away. I was really having a hard time thinking.

"I thought it was neat she'd already written to Imaya." Jessica said. "If it was me I would feel good about that." Like I really needed help from her. At least we were done with that stupid activity, I thought. I was mistaken.

"Now I'd like us to send the stone around again, and mention one thing we would like to have done differently in the past week." Carol said. She went first again and told about how even though she was glad she had expressed her opinion to her friend, she wished she had been more respectful of her friend's feelings while she was speaking up for herself. It made me wonder what they were disagreeing about, but I didn't ask and nobody else did either. It was

Noticing Feelings

Do feelings have colors for you? What shape are they? Are they soft or hard, smooth or jagged? Are they stuck or do they move? Where can you find them in your body?

Danielle's turn and I wondered what she was going to say. She was looking at her hands, her fingernails, really. Finally she said there was one thing she wished she had done differently.

She looked at me in that same strange way. "I'm not going to say what it is right now." She passed the rock to Jessica. Jessica said she wished she had known what to do when she saw Margaret Anderson crying behind the newspaper after the kids were in bed. She just pretended like she didn't see and went to bed.

"Maybe she wanted to be left alone." Danielle said.

"Yes, but maybe she wanted to talk about her husband drowning." Jessica said. Like she would really want to talk to a fat, pimply faced kid who reads fantasy books.

"Margaret must be tremendously relieved to have you there helping her with the children." Carol leaned toward Jessica. "But you are still a child, too. It would be too much to expect you to help her with her grief, Jessica. I don't think Margaret or anyone is expecting you to do that."

"I may be young, but I know what its like to feel sad and alone." Jessica said, hunching forward and hugging herself below her enormous breasts. "Even if no one expects me to, I still wish I could help."

"I think it is great you want to help her," Danielle said. Suddenly everyone seemed to think Jessica was so sweet and wonderful. "If you see her crying again you could give her some tissues to blow her nose, and maybe ask her if she wants some tea. If she starts talking you could just listen like you did with me when we were in our listening pairs. You made me feel like you cared, even though you didn't say anything."

Healing Through Creativity: Spinning Straw into Gold

You may find words or sentences forming in your mind. When you write them down, you have a poem, a story, a rap, or a song.

Jessica nodded. "Thanks, Danielle." She handed the rock to Tara.

Tara pushed her glasses up. "I wish I had tried to talk to Imaya more. I don't know her that well, but I did notice she was by herself a lot. I thought maybe she just wanted to be by herself. I'm no good at talking to people, but now I wish I'd tried."

"Me, too." I said. Danielle and Jessica nodded. Tara handed me the rock. I turned it over and pressed my fingers into its tiny crevices.

"I wish I hadn't slapped somebody." I squeezed the rock until my fingers ached. I needed them to hurt, somehow, to be able to say it. The words came from an inside part of me, the part that maybe Danielle could see. I wished I could sink through the floor. Nobody said anything.

"That's a tough one," Carol said. "Do you want to share any more, Abi?" I squeezed the rock harder. Part of me wanted to say something about my inside feelings and my outside feelings, but I shook my head no. I gave the stone back to

Making a Comfort Box

Making a Comfort Box can help with overwhelming feelings. Sometimes difficult memories or thoughts of wanting to hurt yourself can overwhelm you. When this happens, it helps to have a place to go or imagine going to help you remember about the good stuff in your life, or the things you want to do in the future. If you don't have a plan, it's easy to get lost in the overwhelming feelings. When you have a plan, you can help yourself feel more stable and safe.

To make a Comfort Box, get an empty shoebox or other cardboard box. Next, think of the things that you like to smell, taste, see, hear, and feel. You may be able to put your favorite things right into the box. If they're too big (or if they're people, pets, or otherwise not appropriate to put in a box), you can use pictures of your favorite things. You might consider having a larger box for home, and a smaller one for traveling, especially if you will be gone from home overnight. Below are some ideas to get you thinking about what you might collect that will work for you.[1]

Hmmm ... What Should I Put in My Comfort Box?

Smell: lavender, incense, candles, your favorite aunt's perfume, soap, flowers, bubble bath, freshly cut grass, camp fire, hot chocolate, vanilla, saltwater, garlic, your pet, freshly baked bread. Remember, if you can't package it and put it in the box, any kind of reminder (even a list) will work.

Taste: chicken noodle soup, your mom's famous casserole, fresh oranges, fried chicken, pears, cookie dough, taffy, cotton candy, warm milk.

Sight: photographs of your support people, including friends, family, therapist, school counselor, teachers, foster parents, social worker, etc. Certain colors, or pictures, a drawing of your safe place, pictures of gardens, cottages, stars, laughing babies, and family portraits.

Carol. She looked at my fingers turning white from gripping the stone but didn't say anything. She took a deep breath and let it out. Of course then I felt like taking a deep breath, too.

I was feeling kind of funny inside. Mixed up. I was still angry with Danielle and Jessica on the outside, but on the other hand, I wanted to drop it. I wondered if Danielle wanted to drop it, too. I didn't want to be friends with Jessica, but weirdly enough, part of me still wanted to be friends with Danielle. At the end of the group Carol said she wanted us to make comfort boxes at home to use when we start feeling angry, scared, sad or just plain crummy.

"I could put my puppy in my comfort box," Tara said. "He's soft, he has a nice puppy smell, and he makes me laugh." That made us laugh. Danielle pretended she was the puppy checking out the other things in Tara's comfort box. Carol said that even if we couldn't actually put a certain animal or person or thing in the comfort box, we could include a picture of it, or write its name on a piece of paper.

Hmmm ... What Else Should Go in My Comfort Box?

Sound: your favorite positive music, relaxation tapes, the sound of the ocean in a sea shell, your favorite DVDs, words of affirmation, a tape of your therapist, your mother, or yourself saying calming and soothing words, evening bird songs, rustling leaves, loud music, love songs, crickets, laughter, a cat's purr, falling rain.

Touch: an old blanket from when you were a kid, a piece of your mom's old shirt, a stuffed animal, a letter, a worry stone, brand new socks, flannel.

Other important stuff: names and phone numbers of friends and support people, your personal list of "what to do when I feel like hurting myself," affirmations, special letters or cards, your personal lists of "what makes me happy," "fun and interesting things to do list," and "places to see."

I caught up with Tara on the way out to the lobby and asked if I could come see her puppy. She just looked at me for a moment, and I was afraid she didn't like me, but then she smiled in a very friendly way and said, "Sure." When she drew me a map, I realized it wasn't that far from where I live.

Chapter 13

Bear

After school the next day, I left a note for my mother, and then walked over to Tara's. She was sitting out on the front steps with her puppy. There was a big old dog with long black fur lying on his side in the melting snow near the steps. When I got to the edge of the yard, the puppy came running up to me, all round and wiggly, with his tongue hanging out. I picked him up in my arms and walked over to Tara. The old dog lifted his head to look at me and then laid it back down and closed his eyes.

"He's so cute. What kind is he?"

Tara smiled at me. "His mother is a German shepherd mix and his father is a black lab, but he looks more like his mom." I set the wiggly thing down. Tara picked up a tiny stick and tossed it a few feet away. The puppy ran, stumbled over his feet, ran again, and picked it up in his mouth. We laughed.

"Come, Bear, come here," Tara coaxed, patting her knees. Bear dropped the stick and came running back to Tara. "Good doggie!" She rubbed the puppy's back and sides. "But next time bring the stick, okay?" I laughed again. She looked at me. "Want something to drink?" We went inside, trying not to trip over the puppy.

Nobody else was home. The house was very tidy. I wondered what Tara would think of the messy piles of books and papers at my house. The shelves and windowsills had rows and rows of little tiny statues of dogs and cats. "That's my

mother's collection." Tara said, following my eyes.

"I bet it makes it easy to get her presents."

"Well, sort of, but you'd be surprised. You have to be careful not to get one she already has."

Even though I knew her big brother wasn't living there anymore, I was afraid he would show up. I didn't want to ask her about him. "Where's the rest of your family now?"

"My mom's at the Hospital. She's a nurse's aide. She'll be home around eight. My dad's on the Slope now. He gets back this weekend. He works three on and three off." I was confused.

"You're going to think I'm stupid, but what is the Slope, and what's three on, three off?"

Tara smiled and pushed up her glasses on her nose. "I don't think you're stupid, just not from Alaska. That's where the oil fields are, up by Prudhoe Bay. It's called the North Slope. He drives a road grader up there. He works for three weeks and then he comes home for three weeks."

"I think I get it. Do you have to make dinner when your dad is gone and your mom is working late?"

Tara shrugged. She picked up the puppy and hugged her.

I got the feeling I was asking too many questions. "You're lucky to get to have a puppy. My mom just frowns and shakes her head if I ask about a pet. "Puppies chew and kittens smell,'" I imitated my mom's robot voice, and Tara smiled. "I bet my dad would let me, if it was just him and me. Sometimes I wish I could go back to California with him. We could live near my grandma and grandpa again. I could be with my old friends and nobody would know about what happened with Phil and Jessica and me." Tara was playing with her puppy, and I didn't know what she was thinking, and I couldn't seem to stop blabbering. I sighed.

"Why did you come to Alaska, anyway?" Tara asked.

"My mom was worried about my grandma. She wanted to be close enough to check on her. She's getting confused and she has arthritis really bad. She should be in a nursing home. I don't see why she couldn't have come to California." I made myself stop talking.

Tell Yourself

"I'm safe now," "My feelings are okay," or "I deserve to be loved."

Tara was playing tug of war with Bear with a little piece of rope. Finally she said, "I'd like to go to California. A few years ago, we went to Disneyland. I'd like to go again." She frowned. "But that was before. When we were all together. It wouldn't be the same now. They'd probably have to go without me."

"What do you mean? Wouldn't they leave your brother behind instead of you?"

"I don't know. It seems like everyone blames me for what happened. And everyone likes James. Sammy and Melissa are over at my Aunt's house now, where James is staying. They said they wanted to go play with our cousins, but I know they want to see James."

"Oh Tara, that must feel horrible." Her face was stiff and blank, like she had gone somewhere and forgotten to take her body with her. The puppy nipped her hand.

"Ow! Hey, cut that out." Her face came alive and she whopped Bear gently on the nose.

I laughed. "He sure is playful."

"I bet he's hungry," Tara said, getting up.

Moving with Feelings

Remind yourself that moving with your feelings is healthy.

I looked at my watch. "I've got to get home. Thanks for showing me your puppy."

"Thanks for coming over." Tara was getting a bag of puppy food out of the cupboard. "I'm glad you came."

"Me, too," I said.

On the way home I stopped at a little grocery store to get something to drink. At the checkout counter I picked up a music magazine. There were pictures of Jewel in it. She's from a town in Alaska that isn't that much bigger than Bluff. That is one thing I've always dreamed about … being a popular singer like Celine Dion or Jewel. Everybody says I have a nice voice. The dresses some of the stars were wearing were way sexy. They were like some of the things Phil had me try on. I started feeling weird looking at the pictures. How was I supposed to know it was sexual abuse, when the people I want to be like were doing the same thing?

Sex in Advertising

Sexy, inappropriate, and impossible body images are shown over and over again in commercials and television shows. Often advertisements use sexually suggestive behaviors to sell their products, everything from toothpaste and razors to cars and cell phones. Watching this many sexually loaded ads puts impossible body ideals into your mind and makes you start to feel badly about what your own body looks like.[1]

Chapter 14

The Child Abuse Hotline

I told my father I didn't like it when he patted my bottom. I wasn't actually sure whether I liked it or not, but it made me feel nervous because of when we'd talked about boundaries in the group. I wanted to see what he would say.

"I didn't know it bothered you, Hon. Why didn't you let me know before?"

"It didn't bother me before, Daddy, but, I'm growing up. I'm not your little baby anymore."

"You are growing up." He looked me over from head to toe. "You are turning into a gorgeous woman, Abi." I don't know why, but something about the way he looked at me made me feel uncomfortable. I started wondering about sexual abuse again. I wondered if someone would call that sexual abuse. I wondered if that is why I didn't think what Phil was doing was that big of deal ... because he was looking at me the way my dad sometimes did.

I couldn't sleep that night. I got out the comfort box I was starting to make. There wasn't much in it yet but a couple of CDs, a picture of me and my grandparents in California, and a list of people I want to see again before I die, including most of my friends in California. Looking at that list just made me feel lonely. I tried to practice my piano music in my head, but I just kept seeing my dad behind bars. I tried going to my safe place, the room with all the pillows, but it seemed lonely, too. I wished I could talk to someone.

The next day I had an appointment with my therapist, Jean. When I was in the waiting room I saw a pile of little pamphlets with the words, CHILD ABUSE HOTLINE in big letters. There was a number you could call to talk to someone if you thought you were being abused. The pamphlet explained that since it was an 800 number, there would

When Someone Tells You She Was Abused

■ **Stay Calm:** Getting worked up about what you are hearing is likely to make things more intense. When you're worked up, it's hard to think, and it's hard to hear what the other person is saying.

■ **Be Supportive:** Tell your friend that she is not to blame. She did nothing to make the abuse happen. And that she was right to tell someone about it.

■ **Encourage:** Talk to your friend about where she can go to get help and what it might be like.

■ **Don't Take On Too Much:** Your friend chose to tell you about this because she sees you as someone she can trust, someone she can talk to; but that doesn't mean that you are the only one who can help her. You don't have to take this on all by yourself. Even if you feel like you need to protect your friend's privacy, get some help dealing with the feelings that this may have brought up for you. You can talk to a therapist, parent, or other adult about what you are going through and how it's affecting you.

■ **Don't gossip:** When we gossip about other people's experiences or feelings, we shame them and they may begin to blame themselves for the abuse, become angry, and feel violated (abused) again.

■ Be aware of how you would feel if you were in your friend's shoes.

If one of my friends told me about being abused, I'd be glad they trusted me. Abi

be no long distance charge. It would not even show up on the phone bill if you dial from a regular landline phone. If you dial from a cell phone there might be a charge. I folded up one of the pamphlets and stuffed it in my backpack. 1-800-4ACHILD or 1-800-422-4453.

At first it was hard to talk with Jean, because I was thinking about calling that number. We started making stuff with some clay she has. I wasn't really making much of anything, but it felt good to pound the clay on the table. I told her about what happened with Danielle. Jean wanted to know more about my feelings toward Jessica.

"I'm so scared everyone will think I'm a loser like her. Because we were both abused by Phil." She asked me to talk about what my ideal friend would be like. I played with the clay while I thought about that. Someone who would like me even if they saw me completely, even the parts I keep hidden deep inside, but wouldn't hate me for what I show on the outside. Someone with a sense of humor, who liked music, too. Someone who would like me no matter what other people thought about me. They would know who I really am and care about me.

"Who are you, deep inside?" Jean asked. I liked that question. I liked that Jean wanted to know.

Shame and Fear

Shame is experienced in relationship with others: "What will my friends or my family think of me if they knew about this?" Shame is felt when a person does not have positive support from others, or when a person does not believe that he or she will be supported. As you think about who to share your abuse history with, think about choosing people that you trust and whom you expect to support you. If the person you chose blamed, shamed, or ignored you, try to remember that this response is about the other person's reaction, and not about you.

"On the outside I try to be like the other girls," I said. "I try to fit in and I want people to like me. On the inside I want people to like me too, but it's different. Sometimes what I think just comes popping out from deep inside me and even though I wish I had kept my mouth shut because people might think I'm a creep or a pervert, there it is hanging in the air. I can't take it back. Sometimes I feel like the outside me is a box, and the inside me is trapped inside."

"I'd like you to try to find out what the inside 'you' wants and how she would like her life to be." Jean packed the clay back into the tub, except for my little snake I wanted her to save. "Get a sense of how she would like to be treated. Find out what kind of friends she wants, and how she would like to treat others. Try writing to her in your journal. The inside part and the outside part are both you, Abi."

"I know that," I said.

After we got home I really wanted to call that child abuse hotline number, but I was afraid my mom or dad would hear me. I went upstairs and tried to listen to music, but I couldn't concentrate. Then I went downstairs to practice on the piano, but it was the same thing. My mom came up and gave me a letter. It was from Imaya.

Dear Abi,

Thanks for your letter. This place is okay. I feel safer here. I was acting pretty weird before. It isn't horrible. I miss my mom. I get out soon, probably the beginning of next week. So I won't be at group this week. It will be embarrassing going back to school. I can hear it now: There's Imaya Holmes, the fruitcake. Don't talk to her, she's mental. They (the nurses) are giving me a pill to help me stop washing my hands all the time. You probably heard about that.

Your friend (I hope),
Imaya

P.S. Why were you upset about boundaries? I thought boundaries were between countries.

Dear Imaya,

Thanks for writing back. I know how you feel about school. Everyone at school probably thinks I'm a pervert, after what happened with Phil. I am glad the hospital is okay. If it was me, I would be glad to be away from my mother. She's a witch. Yours must be nicer. I don't think you are mental for washing your hands all the time. Hand washing is healthy. I should do it more often. Does the pill make you not want to do it at all? Don't answer if you don't want to.

I don't know what to say about boundaries. I don't understand them. And that makes me think I might actually be a pervert. Please burn this letter after you read it, okay?
I will miss you at group tomorrow.

Your friend,
Abi

Chapter 15

Trying to Relax

I decided I would try to be less mean to Jessica. Not that I liked her or anything. I just didn't want people to notice anything about her and me together. I was hoping it could be neutral between us, not friends and not enemies. I didn't want Danielle to hate me, but that's not why I made the decision. I said hi to Jessica when we were waiting for my mother to pick us up. She looked surprised. Her hair was clean and she had gotten a haircut. It was layered and fluffy, and somehow it made her face look prettier. When Mom drove up I didn't rush to get into the front seat ahead of her, but she still took the back seat. Mom said hi to both of us and then she started talking, to Jessica, of course.

"What a cute haircut, Jessica," she gushed.

"Thank you, Mrs. Barnes. Margaret cut it for me."

"How is Margaret doing?"

"I guess she's doing okay. The baby is sleeping better."

"How long are you going to live with her?" I asked.

"I don't know. As long as she needs me, I guess," Jessica said, in her quiet voice.

"I'll bet your family misses you," Mom said. Jessica didn't say anything. Maybe they didn't miss her at all. Jessica's parents are probably glad to have her out of the house so they can just enjoy their normal daughter.

Group started with the talking circle again. We were supposed to tell about how our week had gone. Danielle said her father had found out about an eye movement thing on the Internet. She was so excited. She kept hopping up and then sitting down on one leg and then hopping up and sitting down on the other leg.

"Eye movements?" I said, "What do you mean?"

"It's for if you have something bad happen to you and you can't get it out of your head. Not just sexual abuse but people who have been in wars or earthquakes or car wrecks and stuff."

"I don't get it."

"My dad was all exited when he told me about it. It helps you get rid of the really strong ideas that get stuck in your body. Like I keep thinking, "If I fall asleep I'll get killed.' so I can't go to sleep. Even though I know that's probably not true, my body thinks someone will attack me if I fall asleep. Even with all the locks we have on all our doors and windows now, I have a hard time letting myself fall asleep." Carol nodded.

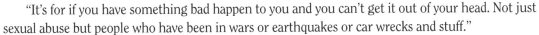

Speak Kindly To Yourself

Use your own name to talk silently to yourself. Tell yourself that you are safe, in the present, and that the abuse is no longer happening.

"EMDR stands for Eye Movement Desensitization and Reprocessing," Carol said. "It helps take the intensity out of the trauma memories. When something very scary and dangerous happens, your body and mind go into a hyper-alert state. Your only focus is on staying alive. You form strong beliefs about what will help you stay alive, such as, 'I must never go to sleep. I'll never be safe in this body.' or 'It is dangerous to be alone.' Then every time something reminds you of what happened, those strong beliefs and all the powerful feelings come rushing back. The eye movement therapy can help with that. It can help your body let go of the strong ideas that won't let you relax. Then you can have more comfortable beliefs like, 'Sleeping is good because it helps me grow strong and heal.'"

Jessica turned to Danielle. "Are you going to do that eye movement therapy?"

Sleep Difficulties

Not being able to go to sleep or stay asleep, being afraid of the dark, and having nightmares are all common experiences following sexual abuse. Sometimes people who have been abused can stop themselves from thinking about the abuse by keeping themselves busy, or by using alcohol, drugs, or food. Using this kind of coping may seem to help for a while, but then the feelings begin to leak or burst out, often in ways that are harder to deal with than if a person hadn't tried to cover the pain. When things are quiet, especially at night when you are more likely to be alone, thoughts and feelings about the abuse might be harder to ignore. It is important to know that this is a normal response to a traumatic experience.

Writing your dreams down so that you feel more in control of them, reading a book, or asking a safe person to read to you until you fall asleep, are all things that might help. Playing soothing music can help too.

Exercising on a regular basis and keeping a regular sleep routine (without naps), will help you to sleep better. Try not to drink coffee or sodas because the caffeine will keep you up at night. Carbohydrates or calcium (cereal, oatmeal, toast, warm milk, sleepy time tea, etc.) right before you go to bed will also help you to sleep better.

What I hate is when you fall asleep fine, but then you wake up in the middle of the night and start thinking about things. Abi

"Yes. There is a guy here in town that does it. We're going to go talk to him tomorrow. I hope he can help me.

"I've heard some great things about that kind of therapy, Danielle," Carol said. "I'm glad you are going to try it. I'll bring a handout next time about different kinds of therapy. There are lots of helpful treatments available these days."

When she said that about trying it, I decided to tell about how when I tried to use my comfort box at home, it didn't work. Carol said she was glad I brought that up because she wanted to check in with us about that anyway.

"I want to talk about that some more today after we all check in."

Jessica told about how she liked staying with Margaret even though they both work really hard taking care of the baby and the little girl.

The children cry a lot, but now the little girl lets Jessica read to her. "I like living with Margaret, because when I walk into the house she looks so happy to see me. At home I felt like everybody was embarrassed I was part of the family." I thought that I would be embarrassed to have her in my family, too. Then I felt sort of odd, tired of myself. I wondered if maybe I should try to stop thinking mean things about Jessica all the time.

Tara told about a chickadee that flew into their kitchen window. She thought it was dead, but when she ran outside and picked it up she could feel its tiny heart beating very fast. She brought it inside and laid it on an old shirt inside a shoebox. After a while she heard it rustling. When she took the box outside and opened the lid the bird flew straight up into the air and away. I wondered why Tara didn't say how things were going with her family. I wondered whether they were going bad or going good.

Carol said she had a good week. She told about her dog getting his foot operated on and having to wear one of those plastic cones on his head so he won't chew on his bandage. Tara was hanging on Carol's every word. She wants to be a vet.

Carol wanted to know if anyone else had tried making and using a comfort box at home and how it had gone. Jessica and Danielle had started making theirs, but nobody else besides me had tried using them yet. Carol wanted to know what I had in my box. She said it was a good start, but it might be good to have a list of friends that are close by, too, not just the ones far away in California.

"Try involving some different senses. What is one of your favorite smells?" she asked.

"I like the smell of my dad making coffee in the morning. Oh, and some perfume a friend gave me."

"Those would be easy," Danielle said. "You could just put the perfume on a cotton ball in little plastic bag."

Carol nodded. "Sometimes no matter what method you try you can't relax. Relaxing just doesn't feel safe," she said.

"When I relax, I'm afraid I'm going to fall asleep," Danielle said, "and if I fall asleep I might get killed. At least that's what it feels like, to me."

Carol nodded again. "If you've had something terrifying happen to you when you were relaxed you may feel that if you

A Few Common Feelings

Confusion:

- Because you love and hate the person who abused you.
- Because you love and hate the people who didn't protect you from being abused.
- Because you wonder what life would be like if you hadn't told.

Guilt:

- Because you could do nothing to stop the abuse.
- Because the abuse may have been pleasurable at times.
- Because someone told you it was your fault.
- Because you were blamed for breaking up the family.
- Because you feel "dirty", "bad", or "different."

Fear:

- That you are not safe.
- That this will never go away.
- That you have been damaged.
- That you are responsible for the fate of the person who abused you.

continued ➤

✎ Anger:

- That cannot be expressed because it is so powerful that it scares you.
- At what has been done to you.
- At yourself.
- At other family members
- At the legal system for the way it has handled the case.
- At the world.
- At God.

✎ Loss of Trust:

- Feeling as if you will never trust anyone again.
- Feeling like you can't trust yourself to make good decisions.
- Feeling that you cannot trust the people who are supposed to protect and love you.
- Feeling scared of letting people get too close to you.[1]

When Jean gave me this handout I started to think that maybe, just possibly, I might be normal. Abi

relax again something bad will happen."

"I try to notice things all the time, now," Tara said. "It's not that I'm afraid of someone attacking me, but I just feel like if I don't pay attention someone might turn out to be different than I thought they were."

"Holding yourself alert and intensely awake all of the time is understandable, but it takes a lot of energy. It is hard on your body. And it probably will not keep you safer in the long run."

"What do you mean?" Tara asked. "If I had paid more attention when James and I were first doing that stuff together, I bet I would have figured out where it was going a whole lot sooner."

Dealing with Big Feelings and Bad Memories

When you are having feelings that overwhelm you or seem to take control, you can distract yourself from them by practicing "grounding" techniques. Grounding just means feeling real, in your body, and in the present moment in a way that feels safe and calm. It helps you to move away from negative thoughts and difficult feelings into a more calm and centered place. [2]

If you start feeling like you're not in your body, spacey, or overwhelmed, look around you and notice something. Describe it to yourself in as much detail as possible. Pay special attention to all the senses in your description. What does the object look like, smell like, feel like, etc. What size and shape is it? What color? This will help bring you back to the present, calm and ground you.

Sometimes I start with my pencil or something that is right in my hand. Abi

Carol smiled and then sighed. "You know more now than you knew then, Tara. You didn't know how it was going to turn out. You can pay attention and keep yourself safe without having your body on red alert 24 hours a day. Being keyed up all of the time will wear you out and make you less able to respond if you have a real danger."

"Maybe that's true, but it doesn't feel that way to me," Danielle said. "Maybe it's like my dad was saying. You can't help thinking it's dangerous to relax because strong ideas about danger get stuck in your body."

Reclaiming Your Body

Sometimes the best type of exercise is an individual type of exercise, rather than a team sport, because you will maintain your own body space in an individual activity. It is important to raise your heart rate, and to begin to feel in control of your body again.

Physical exercise can help you feel less depressed, more confident, and calmer. Some exercises that are particularly helpful include yoga, bellydancing, and karate. Karate and self-defense classes have the added benefit of helping you to feel strong, confident, and in control. You will learn how to get away from someone who tries to hurt you, and how to manage your own body in a way that feels powerful and strong.

Tara and I are going to take Karate together this summer. Abi

Carol nodded. "Even if what I'm saying does not feel true, try to think about it with your whole self, not just the scared part of you. I'm not saying you shouldn't be alert and pay attention to keep yourself safe. I'm just saying your body needs relaxation and play sometimes, too."

Chapter 16

. . . .

Things to Do with Difficult Feelings

Carol stood up to get the big pad of paper and the easel. "Even if you believe it is safe to relax sometimes, you might not want to relax because when you do, uncomfortable feelings and worries start to come up." This sounded familiar. I started playing with a loose thread on my skirt. "So…let's talk about what to do with uncomfortable feelings. Feelings like anger, confusion, guilt, fear, sadness." She wrote "Coping with Difficult Feelings" on top of the page. "Any ideas?" Silence.

"Animals," Tara said. "I take Bear for a walk, or go over to my friend's house and brush her horse." Carol nodded and wrote down "Being with animals."

"I listen to music and sing along or I play the piano. That helps."

"Writing."

"I talk to my mom or my dad or my brother Josh." Danielle said.

"I read a book." Jessica said. Fantasy, I thought to myself.

"Go skiing or jogging." That was Danielle, with her strong little body.

"Call a friend on the telephone." That was me, but I wasn't sure who I would call. Maybe Tara if I got to know her better.

"Eat ice cream," Jessica mumbled, looking ashamed. I made my face blank. I eat ice cream or cookies, too, when I feel crummy, but I wasn't going to say so.

Eating Disorders and Sexual Abuse

If you have been sexually abused, you may have an increased risk of eating in an unhealthy way. Sexual abuse and eating disorders are often connected with feelings of shame and discomfort with one's own body. Problems with eating are common and an understandable reaction to trauma. People who have been abused are often critical of their own bodies, and are more likely to diet or have eating problems than girls who haven't been abused.[1] They often want to have thinner bodies, or the other extreme, to hide their bodies from others. They sometimes believe that if they are not attractive to others they will be less likely to be abused again. This belief leads to a destructive and painful cycle of self-blame and shame and self-harm in the form of the eating disorder. Abuse and eating disorders can both feel very scary and out of control. Eating disorders are a way of saying (without words) that a person feels very out of control but wants desperately to be in control. They may also be a way of taking care of the self (as odd as that may seem to other people, it can be true for the person suffering from an eating disorder), or a way to numb out from feelings.

Carol smiled. "I have to admit, that's one I use, too, Jessica."

"Sometimes I put music on in our TV room and dance." Danielle said. "Well, I like to do that, but usually there is so much junk on the floor in there I don't have room to dance."

"This is a great list," Carol said. "Do any of you do artwork?" None of us did, except Carol. She likes to do bead work, she said, and also drawing, so she put 'make things' on the list. Then she wanted to know which of the things on the list worked best for helping us feel better. Playing piano usually makes me feel better. Eating ice cream is nice while it lasts, but I usually still feel keyed up afterwards.

"Eating makes me feel worse," Jessica said. "It gets my mind off of stuff for a little while, but then I start feeling angry at myself. Even if my mother isn't around, I hear her voice inside me telling me what a fat slob I am."

Carol smiled. "I know what you mean. Some of

us have to learn how to be gentle with ourselves, especially when we're trying to cope with difficult feelings." She flipped another page up on the chart and picked up the marker again. "The way I see it, we have three choices when we notice uncomfortable feelings. 1. Stay with the feelings and try to move with them. 2. Distract ourselves in a healthy way. 3. Distract ourselves in an unhealthy way." She put the pen down.

"Feelings are meant to be dancing, flowing things. They move in us, giving us energy." Carol's hands danced in front of her. "They rise up in us, wave after wave, giving us information about ourselves and things around us. Flowing on, they make room for other emotions. Sexual abuse can interrupt or slow down the natural process of learning to honor and work with our feelings. The confusing and painful feelings from being sexually abused," her hands fluttered wildly like terrified, wounded birds, "can be so intense and overwhelming, we get in the habit of shutting them down and avoiding them."

She clenched her fists against her belly. "It is important to take breaks and distract yourself from feeling painful feelings. No one can stand to hurt all of the time. There needs to be a balance between allowing painful emotions to flow through, and focusing on other things." She smiled apologetically. "I know this is a lot of information. But it is important."

"Knowing how feelings move will help you to relax. If you know uncomfortable emotions are likely to come up when you relax, then you can be prepared. You can have your drawing things next to you, or your friend's phone number, or your music. When feelings come up, you don't have to panic, because you have a plan. Remember to keep breathing, because if you hold your breath the feelings will get stuck. Slow, deep breathing into your belly is best.

If the feelings are too big to deal with alone, you can write yourself a little note so you can remember to talk about them with your therapist or someone else you trust. Then you can distract yourself."

She looked around at us and smiled. "Let's move. I'll give you a handout on it to take home." She had us all stand up and she put on some music. I'd never heard anything like it. There were native voices chanting, with drumming in the background. We were supposed to dance the dances of different feelings, like she had been doing with her hands. First she wanted us to do a dance of laughter, which was a good emotion to have first, because we felt pretty silly.

Then we did an anger dance. I'd never seen so

The Four Most Common Kinds of Eating Disorders

Anorexia: not eating, or eating very little because of a strong fear of fat, food, or calories. A person with anorexia weighs less than 75 percent of his or her ideal body weight. Anorexia can cause enough damage to organs such as the brain, liver, and heart that the person may never be able to live a normal life, and may even die.

Bulimia: eating large portions and then making oneself vomit, over-exercise, or use laxatives to get rid of the food.

Binge eating: eating more than most people would normally eat in one sitting.

Eating Disorder Not Otherwise Specified: eating in a way that is damaging to the body and mind, but does not quite fit any of the above categories.

much stomping and sharp, slashing movements and air punches. Carol kept reminding us to give each other space. The sadness dance was next. I found my arms wanted to make big slow curves. My hips and waist followed my arms in the movements. I dropped my heavy head and arms to the floor, and then rolled up slowly and arched back and to the side moving bleakly, aching inside. Suddenly I realized the music had stopped and the others were just standing there, watching me. I jerked upright, my face on fire. How could they just stand and watch me?

Dance Your Feelings Out

You might want to put on some music and dance a dance of sadness, anger, pain, relief, joy, or love. Dancing is a wonderful way to help feelings move. Dancing can help you feel more at peace with your body. Dance a feeling dance. There is no right way. Notice how your body likes to move.

"That was beautiful, Abi," Danielle said in a hushed voice. I took a deep breath and then started bawling. Carol started up the music again. "Sadness dance, everyone!" She called out and handed me a tissue. I was looking at my feet, and I could see other feet moving around me. I started dancing again, and all the worries about my father and whether he was going to go to jail came up in sobs and shudders. My heart ached and I missed my friends in California, and it felt good to move even though I felt so sad. I am going to call that Hotline number tonight, I told myself. No matter what, I need to know.

"Aliveness dance," Carol called out and started doing a little jig. Danielle and Tara started doing the cancan together and Jessica and I started laughing. Pretty soon we were all in a cancan line dancing around the room.

Chapter 17

Calling the Child Abuse Hotline

We stopped at my grandma's after support group. She was having one of her bad days. Her knees and hip hurt so much she hadn't even gotten out of bed. Mom fixed her a sandwich and brought it in to her. Grandma didn't have much of an appetite, and I could understand why. Her bedroom smelled like someone had spilled a bottle of sweet perfume in a dirty public restroom. I went out into the living room and I tried to work on my homework, but I couldn't concentrate. I just wanted to get home and call that hotline number. Mom and Grandma were arguing in the bedroom. I couldn't understand the words, but I could tell Mom was trying to get Grandma to agree to something and Grandma was absolutely unwilling.

Mom's face was closed when we drove home. I imagined her anger and worry about Grandma crashing around inside of her, trying to flow out. I daydreamed about suggesting she do an anger dance or a worry dance, and watching in horror as she opened her mouth and a noisy tidal wave of feelings came crashing out, washing me away.

Finally, after dinner, when my mom was in her room taking a nap and my dad had gone bowling, I took the phone up to my room. I sat on my bed staring at the phone on my bed. When I finally picked it up, it slipped out of my sweaty hand. I grasped it more firmly and dialed the number on the brochure. "You have reached Childhelp USA's national child abuse hotline." a woman's voice said. "If this is an emergency please hang up and call 911. If you would like to speak with a counselor, please stay on the line." Some music came on for a minute and then the phone went silent. I started to feel sick to my stomach. I remembered about breathing. I put a hand on my belly and let my breath push

What to Do When There Is No Help

Even if there isn't a crisis line in your town or village, there is usually a toll-free number that you can call. It's okay to call, even if you just need to talk for a while. The person who answers the phone will probably understand. Try **1-800-422-4453 (1-800-4ACHILD)**, Child Help USA. You can call 24-7 and it's so confidential that it won't even show up on your phone bill (unless you call on a cell or mobile phone.)

against it. I let my breath out in a long slow hiss. A computer voice came on and said, "If you'd like to make a call, please hang up and try again." Sheesh. It was hard enough doing it the first time. I took two more slow motion belly breaths and then dialed 1-800-422-4453 (1-800-4ACHILD) again. I got the same thing about calling 911, the music for just a few seconds this time, and then a real woman's voice. She sounded friendly, and asked what she could help me with.

"Well, I have a friend, and she didn't want to call you and she asked if I would call for her."

"Okay."

"Uh...she's worried about her dad. She thinks her dad might be abusing her sexually, but she's not sure, and she doesn't want him to go to jail."

"Your friend thinks maybe her dad is sexually abusing her?"

"Yes."

"What is he doing?"

"Well, he just pats her butt."

"He pats her butt?" She sounded concerned.

"Well, not without her clothes on or anything. He just pats her butt the way he used to do when she was a kid, but now she feels uncomfortable about it."

"How old is your friend?"

"Thirteen."

"Have you encouraged your friend to talk to her dad about it and tell him how she feels?"

"She did ask him not to do it anymore, and he stopped doing it. But now he looks at her and says things like, 'You are turning into a beautiful young woman' and the way he looks at her makes her feel weird."

"The person your friend really needs to be talking with is her dad. She should sit down with her dad and her mom and let them know how she is feeling. She's growing up now, getting into adolescence and she needs to let him know that what he is doing is making her

Personal Space and the Hula Hoop

If you are unsure of your own personal space requirements, or if you are comfortable with very close distances between you and another person, it may help to know that the majority of people in America feel comfortable with about a hula hoop's distance between them and another person. Imagine (or try it out with a real hula hoop) standing in the middle of a hula hoop; most people's comfort zone goes right to the edge of the hula hoop, or about 18 inches from where you're standing. When someone comes closer than that, they start to feel crowded. Even if you are comfortable with smaller distances, it is important to respect the space requirements of others, which may be wider than yours.

If you feel comfortable only with very large spaces between you and another person, either physical or emotional, it may help to work with a therapist, who can help you begin to feel safer and more comfortable.

feel uncomfortable. And of course, you can give your friend this number and encourage her to give us a call directly and talk about it."

"Is what her dad is doing sexual abuse?"

"No." She said it clearly and surely, as if there was no question about it. I thanked her and hung up. My heart was pounding in my chest. I lay back against my pillow. I took slow deep breaths. I felt that "No" warming and soothing me like a thick wool blanket on a cold day. I felt more and more cozy and tired. I woke up in the middle of the night and crawled under the covers.

Chapter 18

Jake

Jake had been trying to talk with me, but I'd been avoiding him. He came up to me at my locker and wanted to give me a Pepsi. I just looked at him and shook my head.

"Come on, Abi, give me a chance," he said. "I'm sorry if I hurt your feelings. I didn't mean to." He combed his fingers through his brown hair so it stood up in tufts. He leaned closer to me, and this time I didn't pull away. "I'm sorry I laughed about that thing with that youth pastor," he said softly. "I was just embarrassed. I'm sorry."

I could feel my face getting hot. I stuck my head into my locker and pretended I was trying to find something in my coat pocket. Why did people think the school hallway was a good place to talk to me about being sexually abused? When I pulled my head out Jake was walking away. I picked up the can of Pepsi down by my feet.

"Thanks, Jake." I whispered.

After school I had an appointment with Jean. I always felt good when I was walking into her office and seeing the shelves full of art supplies, games, and toys. The cozy chairs and couches with bright pillows were like her warm smile. I knew exactly what I wanted to do ... play with clay and talk about my dad. I told her I had been worried about him going to jail for patting my butt and looking at me that way. She laughed when I told her about saying that it was my friend with the questions for the hotline counselor. "It was brave of you to call, Abi."

Let Feelings Fuel Your Creative Fires

Try acting out or showing your feelings with toys, stories, dance, music, sounds, facial expressions, writing, or artwork.

"I had to talk to someone!"

"What do you think about what the counselor suggested, talking to your father and mother?" she asked, making tiny yellow petals.

I mixed together some red and black. "My parents would get mad at each other, I bet. My mom already hates my dad."

"Hates him?"

"She's always mad at him for something. Seems like she is mad at him for being alive. She's mad at everyone right now."

"So you're afraid that if you talk to them, she'll blow up at both of you?"

"Yeah, and I don't want my dad to be mad at me, too. It's bad enough with my mom."

She nodded. "Tell me more about you and your dad."

I rolled the marbled red and black clay into a ball. "I love my dad. He cares about me and thinks I'm neat. He likes being with me. Not like my mom. She walks around in a dark cloud of aggravation. If she notices me, it's only to send out a lightening bolt." Jean gave a half smile, but her eyes were caring. I tore off bits of the ball and rolled them into smaller balls. "It's just that sometimes the way my father looks at me and talks to me reminds me of how Phil was with me!"

Jean nodded. "Just because a person is interested in you and likes you and thinks you are beautiful doesn't mean he or she is going to sexually abuse you. Fathers sometimes get kind of mixed up about how to relate to their daughters when they start to grow up." I didn't say it out loud, but she was giving me the creeps. I thought parents were supposed to know what they are doing; after all, they're the adults. Jean seemed to be reading my mind. "Even

Moving With Feelings: Anger

Hitting a ball with a racket can feel good when you're angry.

Focusing on Your Heart

If you have a bad memory that keeps pushing into your mind, and you can't get rid of it, here is something fun you can try which may help take the intensity or power away from the memory.

Focus on your heart. Breathe slow and deep. Think about a time when you felt a heart-warming emotion such as love, joy, or gratitude. Remember how you felt at the time, and let yourself re- experience that emotion. Keep noticing your heart. You are likely to feel a pleasant warm or wide feeling or sensation arising in and around your heart along with the feeling of love, joy, or gratitude. Let the pleasant sensations flow out to the rest of your body. Stay with the pleasant sensations as long as you want.

If you want to, you can look at the bad memory again, but first pretend there is a little version of yourself sitting in your heart in the middle of all those pleasant sensations. You may want to imagine that an angel or power animal or someone you love and trust is sitting or standing very close to you inside your heart. Then look at the bad memory from inside your heart. Imagine that it is far away, or behind a screen.[1]

if your dad doesn't have everything figured out, it isn't fair for him to treat you like a girlfriend. If he is doing that, it's not sexual abuse, but it's not a good thing."

"What do you mean, if he's doing that? I told you what he does."

Jean nodded. "He notices how beautiful you are becoming, he enjoys your company, and he seems to be more comfortable with you than he is with your mother right now." She paused. "Abigail, if your father is making sexual comments about your body, that could cross over the line into sexual abuse."

"No," I said. "No, he hasn't done that, really."

I thought for a beat or two. "I want him to be interested in me, but it does feel kind of weird that he is way more interested in me than he is in my mom." I smashed all my little balls into pancakes with my thumb. "It makes me feel almost like I'm better than her. That makes me feel awful."

"You get caught in the middle."

"Yeah." I decided to make petals, too. "I feel better just talking about it. Maybe I'll talk to them about it. Maybe I won't."

"Let me know how it goes."

I almost skipped out of her office that day, I felt so light. It helped so much just knowing someone else understood how mixed up I feel about Dad.

Imaya is back in school. She wasn't in the cafeteria at lunchtime, but I saw her in the hallway between classes. She walked the same, tall and striding with her hips forward and her shoulders back, like a model or a movie star, but something about her was different. When I called to her she turned to me with a startled expression for a second, as if she was surprised to see me there. Then she smiled and seemed like herself again. We didn't have time to talk.

Jake asked me to go to the movies with him on Sunday. I said I'd check with my parents. I did want to go with him. I just hoped he wouldn't say anything more about the sexual abuse.

Chapter 19

What To Do If You Feel Like Hurting Yourself

When Jessica and I came in to the group room on Thursday, Imaya was curled in the blue beanbag chair, hugging her long legs in front of her chest. I plopped down on the end of the couch near her.

"I'm so glad you're back."

"Me, too," Jessica echoed. Imaya gave us a little smile. Everyone else was already there. Carol gave us the handout about different kinds of therapy she had promised us.

We looked at the handout for a few minutes. I figured I was in at least four kinds: talk therapy, art therapy, individual, and group therapy. Plus the movement stuff we do in this group. I wondered if doing so much therapy stuff means I have a mental problem, but I didn't say anything.

Carol got the river rock out and handed it to Danielle for her to check in. Imaya was next. I was hoping Imaya would talk about being in the hospital, but I didn't want her to feel embarrassed about it.

"You're all probably wondering about me being mental," she said, when Danielle handed her the stone.

"You're not mental," I said. The others nodded.

"Well I was in a nut house."

Carol took one of her deep breaths and let it out. "There's a lot of prejudice about psychiatric hospitals. They're just places where people can get lots of help and support for coping with feelings that have become overwhelming. And certainly, when someone has been terrorized and abused, of course it's difficult to cope. It would be abnormal not to be

Avoiding the Feelings Caused by Sexual Abuse

Many people want to avoid the uncomfortable feelings that dealing with sexual abuse causes.*

You might be thinking, "Why should I think about it?" or "I just want to forget about it" or, "It's over with. I just want to get on with my life."

The problem with doing this is that the feelings may stay locked inside for a long time, but they will eventually begin leaking out, usually before you even realize it. When you avoid the feelings you may start having flashbacks, nightmares, or body memories. You might start to think you are going crazy, but this is really only a natural reaction to avoiding strong feelings and memories.

Sometimes when these experiences start to happen, people avoid things even more by using drugs or by hurting themselves. Even though it is painful and difficult, working through the feelings you are having so that you can go on with your life and truly leave the abuse behind you can be very rewarding. Once you deal with the feelings, the abuse can become another part of your life experiences, not something that defines who you are.

*duh! Abi.

having a hard time. That doesn't mean you are crazy, Imaya."

"It's crazy to feel like you have to wash your hands a hundred times a day or something horrible is going to happen. It's crazy to do this." She pushed up her sleeves. I opened my mouth and closed it quickly. Her arms were covered with cuts and scabs.

"Sometimes hurting yourself is a way of trying to handle difficult feelings, a kind of mixed up way of protecting yourself," Carol said, gently. "And thinking about washing your hands all the time can take your mind off of terrifying memories." Imaya started crying quietly. Carol handed the box of tissues to me and I pressed one into Imaya's hand. Her face looked limp and puffy. I remembered how I used to notice her jaw muscles making hard ridges under her skin. I wanted to leave. I wanted to get away from her; the change made me feel so sad and strange.

"Oh Imaya," Jessica said. "If you're mental, then so am I. Look at me, wearing these huge jeans and they are already too small. When I get nervous or sad I just eat and eat. It keeps my mind off of things, but it's disgusting." I had a hard time seeing how that was going to make Imaya feel better.

Danielle nodded. "Lately, when I've been feeling really anxious I get into my dad's whiskey. Once I got really drunk. I'm scared that I'm an alcoholic. After the first time I told myself I'd never do it again. But I've done it ..." she looked confused, like she couldn't remember how many times. Then she mumbled, "I hope I never do it again."

"It has been helping — what we talked

Things to Do When You Feel Like Hurting Yourself

If the first one doesn't help enough, try another and another until something does help.

- Call your therapist.
- Call a friend.
- Tell a trusted adult that you're having a hard time being alone.
- Call the child abuse hotline.
- Do a feeling dance.
- Take a deep belly breath and let it out slowly three or four times.
- Say "I'm safe now" or "My feelings are okay."
- Go for a swim.
- Play with your dog.
- Make a picture.
- Write to a friend.
- Write to an enemy and burn the letter (safely!).

continued ➤

Things to Do When You Feel Like Hurting Yourself (con't.)

- Write or talk to yourself.
- Write about how you're feeling.
- Remember that feeling this way doesn't mean you're crazy.
- Remember that feelings move and change and you won't always feel this way.
- Jump rope.
- Make up a song.
- Play the piano.
- Volunteer.
- Write a poem.
- Redecorate your room.
- Stomp your feet.
- Think about people you love.
- Scream out loud.
- Scream louder.

- Take a bath.
- Go to your safe place.
- Paint your nails.
- Exercise.
- Light a candle.
- Hold an ice cube on your wrists or stomach.
- Look in your Comfort Box.
- Go for a walk.
- Look at the lists you have created.
- Make something with clay.
- Tear up old magazines or phone books.
- Watch a funny movie.
- Look at nature.
- Surround yourself with beauty.

Making Lists Can Be Helpful

Making lists is one way to help remind yourself of the good things in life when you can't remember one good thing. Lists can be stored in your Comfort Box so that you can get them out and look through them when you are feeling down.

about last time." Jessica said. "You weren't here, Imaya, but we talked about things to do if you're having really uncomfortable feelings. I've been trying to write instead of eat."

"Maybe we could make a list, a plan, and then Carol could copy it for us. Things to do if we are feeling like hurting ourselves." Danielle was bouncing up and down on the couch, her face pink, and her eyes shining.

Carol smiled at her. "That's a great idea, Danielle. When you are feeling very upset, it's hard to think. It helps to have something already figured out. If someone will write it out by hand, I can make copies for you before you go today." I volunteered, since I have good handwriting.

"Thanks for being so nice, you guys," Imaya said. Her face looked a little better. "It's not like I'm actually feeling all these feelings when I do that stuff." She pulled the sleeves of her sweatshirt down over her hands. "I just feel sort of numb. It's like I've got to do it or something horrible will happen."

"What will happen?" Tara asked.

"I don't know. I don't want to know ... something really bad ... too horrible to think about."

"Sounds like you need to do some pretty powerful things to help you keep those thoughts at bay," Carol said.

"What do you mean?"

"The hand washing and cutting yourself is working. It is helping you keep from thinking about something that feels too scary."

"It's NOT working." Imaya almost yelled. She looked startled, and then said

Be a Friend to Yourself
Use the tools from your Comfort Tool Box.

Substance Abuse and Sexual Abuse

Lots of teenagers and children experiment with alcohol and drugs. Sometimes they even get caught up in drinking and using in ways that are harmful to their health and relationships. People who have been sexually abused, though, may use drugs and alcohol for different reasons than other teens.

Many girls and boys who have been sexually abused use alcohol or drugs to deal with the feelings related to abuse. Many adults who go through treatment to help them stop using alcohol or drugs have been sexually abused as children.[1] Sometimes their use of alcohol or drugs started when the offender gave them alcohol or drugs in order to make them easier to abuse.

Alcohol and drugs offer a way of escaping from the feelings, thoughts, and memories of abuse (if you numb out when using), or as a way of allowing yourself to feel (if you usually are cut off from your feelings). Because sexual abuse survivors often want to change their feeling state, they may skip past the experimentation phases of alcohol and drug use, and become addicted more easily than others.[2]

Substance abuse creates its own problems and makes the abuse more complicated to deal with. If you feel substance use is a problem for you, find someone who is willing to help you get help.

Sometimes I just want to escape everything. Abi

more quietly, "That's the thing. I have to do it more and more. I can't do anything else because it takes up all my time. I can't stand to be in school because that dread starts overtaking me and I just have to leave so I can do that stuff."

"What's going on in your life, Imaya?" Carol asked.

"What do you mean?"

"What is happening with you and your mom?"

"Well, nothing much. We're still living in the apartments next to the Women's Shelter, but my mom's got a job now. We have to move out into a regular apartment next month. Where we are living now is what they call transitional housing. It's really low rent and the counselors from the Shelter check on us a lot." She pulled at her sleeves and then jumped up. "I gotta go." We watched her almost run out of the room.

I used to envy her, so tall, dark and beautiful. She seemed powerful, and above it all. Not mixed up like me. I wrote, "Things to Do if I Feel like Hurting Myself" in big letters across the top of the note pad Carol had given me. It was quiet.

When a Parent Has Been Abused as a Child

When a parent has his or her own history of sexual abuse, it may be difficult for him or her to be completely available to the child.

- The parent may over-identify with the child's situation, causing strong memories and thoughts about his/her own abuse that stops them from being able to comfort or nurture their child.

- If the parent blames themselves for the abuse that happened to them, the parent may appear angry or blaming toward the child. If the parent has a severe history of sexual abuse, it is possible that he or she may even blank out when seeing signs of abuse. Fears about survival might stop the parent's brain and senses from working well. They may forget things they see or hear. The parent may not even be able to hear it when the child clearly tells them about the abuse.

- When a parent has strong feelings of guilt or responsibility they sometimes minimize or ignore the child's disclosure of abuse. These types of reactions can be devastating to the child, who looks to parents for love, support, and protection. The reaction of the child can be to blame themselves, to "recant," (say that the abuse never happened) or to doubt themselves and their sanity.

If your parent seems unable to support or protect you, please seek help from another adult.

When a Family Needs an Abuser's Income to Survive

Sometimes a family needs the money that the abusive parent, step-parent, or boyfriend makes to pay for food, clothing, and a place to live. When this happens, it may be difficult for the non-abusing parent to stand up to the abuser and stop the abuse.

If this is happening to you, telling an adult outside your immediate family can help. They can help your family find organizations that will provide food, clothing, money for survival, and a place to live while stopping a pattern of abuse.

I'm thinking of working in an abuse shelter when I'm older. I want to really make a difference. And besides, I already know quite a bit about abuse. Abi

Everyone watched me. Imaya came back in and sat down quickly, not looking at anyone.

Carol took one of her deep breaths and let it out. "So you and your mom are going to be moving out of transitional housing soon. Do you have a place to go?" Imaya didn't answer, just looked down at where she was hiding her hands in her sleeves. I wondered why Carol couldn't see she was making Imaya uncomfortable.

"Let's work on our list." I said, holding up the note pad.

Carol smiled at me. "Just a minute, Abi." She looked back at Imaya.

"I'm afraid she'll move in with him." Imaya whispered.

Carol couldn't hear her so I said, "She's afraid they'll move in with him." I looked at Imaya. "With your stepfather?"

Imaya nodded. "Mom says no, she isn't going back to him, but I can't stop worrying about it. He is going to get out of jail in May. I think she will change her mind and go back like she did before. That's what I mean. I'm crazy."

"If that's crazy, I'm crazy," Danielle said. "I'm always worrying about stuff people say isn't going to happen. I can't ever believe I'm safe."

"All these feelings and behaviors you girls have been talking about today are very common for kids who have been hurt. Sexual abuse is always confusing and sometimes terrifying. Coping with the intense feelings by eating too much, using alcohol or drugs, or injuring yourself in some way isn't healthy, but it's not crazy. You're doing the best you can." Carol smiled at all of us. "But moving with the feelings and getting support when you need it, that's what will help you feel better in the long run." She looked at her watch. "Let's work on that list."

After we made the list we gave each other our phone numbers. I didn't even mind giving mine to Jessica for some reason. If she called when she was feeling bad I would try to help, but I figured she probably wouldn't call me anyway.

Chapter 20

Tara and I Talk

I went over to Tara's again on Saturday. Her little brother and sister were watching cartoons and her mom was stretched out on the couch reading a newspaper. She smiled at me and said hi. Tara seemed eager to get out of the house, so we took Bear for a walk. At the end of her road we cut through the woods on a moose trail to a bigger path along the river. The path was a little muddy and there were still big piles of snow here and there. Clouds went in front of the sun and I zipped my jacket up high around my neck.

"This is nice," I told Tara. "I've never been back here."

"I come here all the time."

"Look at Bear!" The puppy's whole face was under a pile of snow, snuffling after something.

Tara started giggling and then I started laughing. We couldn't seem to stop. Bear pulled his head out and jumped up on our legs, barking his little puppy bark. We ran down the path and he came yipping after us until finally Tara turned around and scooped him up by his muddy little puppy belly.

"I used to come down here with our old dog, Butler, but he got so slow. Now he doesn't even want to walk with me anymore. He barely lifts up his head when I go out the door."

"Thanks for taking me here."

When You Feel Your Friend's Pain

When you hear someone else talk about their abuse you may have your own strong feelings about it.

When you get really close to someone, you can start to take on their feelings, thoughts, and even start to talk or act like them. This can happen to close friends, and it can also happen in groups of friends.

When you have been through similar things you might form a kind of group identity that binds you together and makes you feel like you know each other better than anyone else can ever know you.

Being close to someone is wonderful, but sometimes it can also get scary. When a person realizes that they want to separate from a friend or a group of friends, but they don't know how to do it, life can feel pretty confusing.

Remember that the other person's story isn't your story — and breathe deep into your belly. Their life isn't your life — and exhale your breath. You have the right to have your own thoughts and feelings — and breathe; in through your nose, out through your mouth. Let your breath out slowly and with purpose.

When you really feel stuck and you are overwhelmed with listening to someone else's story, you might even imagine a big magnet over your head, pulling your feelings back to you and another magnet over their head, pulling their feelings back to them.[1]

"Sure." I was listening to the river, dreaming about having my piano by the river on a warm summer day and playing a duet. Tara's voice startled me.

"I can't decide whether or not to go to my Aunt's tonight."

"What do you mean?"

"She's having a party. My mom's other sister and her family are visiting from Martin's Pass. I want to see them, but I don't want to be around them if they find out about James and me. If they don't already know about it, I know someone will tell them. I know they will blame me for what happened."

"That is so stupid. How can they blame you?"

"Come on, Abi." Tara stopped in the trail. "People do." She looked at me and then down at Bear at her feet. I remembered Jake laughing and saying, "I didn't know you were that kind of girl, Abi." The memory made my stomach churn.

"It is different with me," I said. Tara didn't say anything, just turned, and started walking down the path again.

"He didn't pressure me," I told her hunched back. "I could have left. It's different with you. You didn't have any choice. He was bigger than you and five years older. You were trapped. And then you told your mom about it, anyway. You had courage."

Tara stopped and turned around. She was shaking her head slowly and almost smiling. "It's funny, Carol keeps trying to tell us about how sexual abuse is not our fault and we didn't cause it, and we can still only believe it for each other."

> **Myth:** Once you've healed, feelings from the sexual abuse will never bother you.
>
> **Fact:** Healing happens in spurts. You heal as much as you need to at the time, and then you do other things. Later, you might need to do more healing work. For example, if you were abused as a young child, you may need to do more healing when you start having your period, or again when you have a child of your own. Painful feelings from the past may wait to come to the surface until you feel strong enough and have enough support to deal with them. One part of healing means knowing when and how to distance yourself from painful feelings, and when and how to allow them to flow through you and heal you.

"What do you mean?"

Tara reached down and scooped her whining puppy up. "You got tricked and used by an adult pervert, who is in jail now. I can see that isn't your fault, but you feel like it is."

I almost laughed as I saw what she meant. "And you got molested by your brother who is bigger and stronger than you and who threatened you. I can see that wasn't your fault, but you think it was."

Tara grinned at me. "I'll race you back to the house."

"I can't run very well," I yelled, but she had already taken off, Bear barking at her heels. She waited for me out by the road.

"Listen," I panted, "if you don't want to go to that party tonight, come over to my house."

"Thanks. I might. I'll call you." I was glad to see she was breathing hard, too.

Chapter 21

. . . .

We Learn About Sticking Up for Ourselves

At group the following Thursday, Carol said we were going to be learning how to stick up for ourselves. The first step in sticking up for yourself is noticing how you feel and what you want, she told us. According to Carol, once you know what you want, it is easier to ask for it.

"Think back to last week when we made the list of things to do if you feel like hurting yourself. Lots of the activities on that list will help you get more clear about how you feel and what you want." She looked at each of us. "But sometimes just feeling the feeling isn't enough. For example, after you let anger or fear flow through, you may realize you need to do something to stick up for yourself."

"I know exactly what you mean!" Imaya sat forward on the edge of the couch. "After the group last Thursday, I told my mom I just couldn't stand it if we moved back in with Eddie. I told her I would run away or kill myself if we did." Imaya clenched her fists, then opened her hands and pulled her sleeves down over her fingers. "She wanted to know where I got the idea that we might move back in with him. I reminded her about last time when she promised we wouldn't go back. Then, after we couldn't afford groceries and Eddie was giving her flowers and begging her to come back, we did. She said that was different, that sometimes mothers can do things for their kids they can't do for themselves. Last time, when she went back to Eddie, she didn't know he was abusing me, too. And she said she has gotten a lot of help and support and is a lot stronger than she was then." Imaya sighed and tucked her hands under her legs. "Anyway, she said if she can't find an apartment we can afford by the time we have to move out of Transitional

What Are Your Absolutes?

The first part of speaking up for yourself is knowing what you want and what you need. It can be helpful to think about your emotional boundaries and your personal space boundaries when you first start to think about assertiveness.

One way to do this is to take an issue that you struggle with, for instance, saying no to drugs or alcohol, or deciding whether to ride in a car with friends. Think about that issue and decide what your "absolutes" are. Your absolutes are those things that you will absolutely do or absolutely not do. If you know that you will never use drugs with someone you don't know, never do a certain kind of drug, or never ride in a car with someone who has been drinking, that can help you to determine what the things are that you are most willing to stand up for. If you have never thought about how far you are willing to go, or when you want to stop something, you are more likely to do something that you won't feel good about later.

Housing she will ask for an extension."

"Good for you, Imaya," Carol said. "You really did stick up for yourself."

"I still don't totally believe her, but some part of me does. When I feel like I have to cut myself, I run pictures in my head like a movie, over and over again, of her looking at me, all powerful like a mother tiger, and saying she is stronger now and if she needs to, she'll get an extension. It does help some."

"Do you think they really would give you an extension at that housing place?" Danielle asked. I couldn't believe she asked that. I was afraid Imaya would get all worried again.

Imaya smiled. "I went over and asked a lady I know in the main office. She said they would."

"Go, Imaya!" Carol said, and everyone started cheering and clapping. Imaya grinned and flexed first one bicep and then the other. We laughed until my face hurt. Finally, Carol asked if any of us had examples of ways we had spoken up for ourselves, or of things we'd like to stick up for ourselves about. I thought about talking to my parents about how I don't like it when my dad treats me like a girlfriend. I didn't really want the other girls to know about it.

What Are Your Absolutes? (Cont.)

Once you have determined what your absolutes are, you can think about the areas in between. It is sometimes useful to think about the in between areas with a therapist, a friend, or a trusted family member who can help you think about all the possible consequences and complications. Once you know your wants and needs (your absolutes and the grey areas in between), you are well on your way to being more assertive.[1]

Tara pushed her glasses up. "I wish I could stick up for myself with my cousins. Last Saturday there was a party at my Aunt's house and I didn't even go." She wanted help with what to say if one of her cousins started blaming her for James getting kicked out.

"I have a handout on that." Carol passed it out.

Carol had Tara act like she was one of the cousins. Carol pretended she was Tara. "You think it's my fault James has to stay with Aunt Leena. That's not the way I think about it. I have rights and he broke the law. The way I see it, James is lucky he didn't get sent to youth prison, or a home for juvenile delinquents."

Tara started giggling, then stopped herself. "James says you led him on and you wanted it. He says that you were no victim."

Carol raised her eyebrows. "So that is what he is saying. The truth is that he pressured and threatened me."

Tara's lips were white. "You're just a slut." She tucked her head and started crying, the tears pooling on her lenses. "I don't want to even talk to any of them. They probably do think what James is saying is true."

I gave her a tissue. "He's full of it."

Carol sighed. "No one wants to believe that a boy they know and love would make his sister be sexual with him."

"They just wish I would shut up about it," she sobbed. "They don't care if it happens as long as nobody talks about it. They think I'm a slut and that I betrayed my brother."

"Do any of your relatives support you, Tara?" Carol asked.

Tara took her glasses off and dried them with the bottom of her sweatshirt. "My mom does, of course, and my dad,

Responding to Someone Who is Blaming You for Something that Is Not Your Fault

Try to stay calm. Take some slow deep breaths into your belly. Remember that you have your own point of view. Listen to what the other person is saying while imagining a shield that protects you from any poisonous or hurtful words.

Try to put what the other person is saying in your own words and say it out loud. This will help you calm down, let the other person know you are listening, and remind both of you that it is just one point of view. For example: "You think that if I hadn't told the school counselor Mom was abusing me, she wouldn't be in jail now, and our family would still be together. And you feel like it's my fault we are in foster care now." Try to keep your tone of voice neutral rather than blaming. Give your own point of view, trying to avoid blaming others. For example: "I don't see it that way. Abuse is against the law. I couldn't stand it anymore. I needed help and I didn't know where else to turn."

If the other person is listening, and you feel safe enough, you might want to share more of your feelings. "I miss Mom, too. I feel so alone."

If the other person continues to attack you or tries to make you feel badly, avoid showing your feelings. State: "I disagree with you about this." or "I have a different point of view." or "I don't see it that way." Then move away from the critical person and get help from someone who will listen to you.

I like to think about whether or not certain people would listen to me if I disagreed with them. Abi

too. I think Aunt Leena does, but she doesn't really talk to me much." She blew her nose again. "My cousin, Theresa, is nice to me. She's older than me. She told me she got molested by our Uncle Leroy. That's my mom's brother, Leroy, who lives in Fairbanks now."

"Maybe you could stay with one of those people, if you are at a party." I said.

Tara looked at me and nodded. "Sometimes I wish my puppy, Bear, were really a bear ... a big grizzly bear that came with me everywhere. Nobody would mess with me. If anyone said anything I didn't like, he would growl."

"Maybe the bear is your power animal." Danielle said. "Have you heard of that?" Tara shook her head.

I couldn't help watching Danielle's hair jiggle as she started her excited little bounce. "Everybody has their own power animal. They help you. Like if you dream about a certain animal that might be your power animal. Or if you are out walking and you see that animal when you are thinking about a problem it might be trying to help you. I have some cards at home that tell about the different animals, what they mean. I can look up the bear for you."

Imaya looked doubtful. "Last night I had a nightmare about spiders. Does that mean they are my power animals?"

"I don't know," Danielle said. "A nightmare, huh?" She wrapped one of her ringlets around her finger. "Spiders are about creating, Imaya. If the spider is your power animal, it can like help you create the kind of life you want."

"Yeah, right." Imaya frowned.

"Danielle has a point," Carol said, "In some traditions it is Spider woman who creates the universe." She shrugged, "but we all come from different cultural groups and we each have our own personal history. What feels healing and supportive to one person might feel frightening to someone else." Then she told us that she personally believes we all have helpers and guides. "Whether you think of them as power animals, or angels, or spirit guides, I believe nobody is ever truly alone."

Chapter 22

Sticking Up for Myself

I went up to my room after dinner. I was thinking about what Carol had said about everyone having guides and helpers. There was a picture in our hallway of a little girl crossing a bridge with a huge friendly looking angel watching over her. Wherever we have lived, my mother has always put that picture up near my room. I wondered if I really did have a guardian angel or a power animal or maybe both. I decided to ask my angel or my power animal to be with me when I talked with my parents. It had become horribly clear to me that I wasn't going to be able to put off talking with them even one more day.

Mom was at the kitchen table sorting through some paperwork, probably my grandma's. She looked irritated when I told her I wanted to talk to her and Dad about something. But she got up and came into the living room with me. I hadn't seen my mother smile in weeks. Dad was in his recliner reading a magazine, but he put it down and lowered his footrest when we came in together. It must have surprised him to see Mom and me doing anything together.

"I want to talk to you and Mom." I sat down on the couch on the end closest to Dad and Mom sat on the other end so the three of us made a little triangle.

"Sure, Honey," my dad said, looking concerned.

"It's just that it makes me feel weird…" I sighed. "I don't like it when…" Finally, I blurted, "Sometimes it seems like you wish I was your girlfriend instead of your daughter and it makes me feel weird." My mom gasped. I wished I could disappear.

Dad looked angry. "You are my daughter, Abi. I don't know what you are talking about."

"Is your father molesting you, Abi?" my mother asked in a tense voice.

"No!" I shook my head. "No. He used to pat my bottom but when I asked him to stop he did. It's just that he always wants to be with me and talk to me about his work and have me rub his neck. It makes me feel funny because he only talks to me, not you."

My mother's face looked stiff, like it might break. It was the color of the ivory piano keys. My dad's face and arms were fiery red. "Is this something you've been discussing in your so called support group? Or maybe you've been talking about this with your therapist, Abi?" He sounded hurt and angry at the same time.

"No, Dad." I was afraid to say I had talked about it with Jean or the hotline counselor.

My mother turned to me and tried to smile. "It is good you brought this up, Abi. I think your father and I need to talk about this now." She meant I should leave. I got up. I wanted Dad to look at me, to let me know it was okay, but he was looking at her.

I didn't want to hear what they were saying. I put my earphones on and turned up the volume and lay on my bed. I couldn't stop crying. After a long while I felt the front door slam, then my mother's footsteps up the stairs, and knocking on my door. I didn't answer, but she came in anyway. I pretended I didn't hear her. When she sat down on my bed and put her hand on my ankle, I finally looked at her.

If You're Scared…
Think about
your safe place.

> ### A Voice for Your Feelings
> When strong feelings come up, you may feel like making noises. Sometimes noises that come from a powerful place deep within your core can be scary. Tears may come, or laughter. If you can allow yourself to go with the feelings and noises, instead of resisting them, you will be able to heal more fully and quickly.

Her watery eyes looked red and ugly against her white face. "Your father is going to go back to California for a while."

I jumped out of bed. "What!" I shouted.

"We need a break from each other, Abi. We both knew it, but what you said tonight helped us see it more clearly."

"He didn't even say good bye to me!"

"He is staying in a hotel tonight."

"You can't do that. He's my father!" I screamed. "Get out of my room! I hate you, you mean bitch! This is all your fault." Her face turned even paler and she was yelling something at me, but I couldn't hear because I was shouting at her to get out. Finally she did. I cried myself to sleep, but at four in the morning I was wide-awake thinking about all the people I was angry at. My father, for leaving me. My mother, for being such a bitch that he left her. The hotline counselor who said I should talk to my parents. Jean, who didn't warn me about what might happen. Carol, for saying we should speak up for ourselves. My stupid guardian angel, if I even had one, for letting this turn out so horribly. Myself, for being stupid enough to talk to my dad with my mother listening. My parents were breaking up and it was my fault.

When my mom came knocking at my door a few hours later I told her I had a stomachache and I wouldn't be going to school. She said she was planning on letting me stay home anyway so I would have a chance to say goodbye to my dad.

"What do you mean?" I mumbled into my pillow.

Scream
Find a safe place to go ahead and scream out loud. Scream out louder.

"He is planning to stop by before his plane leaves, if that's okay with you." I didn't say anything. It wasn't okay that he was leaving me here in Bluff with my witch mother. It wasn't okay that his plane was leaving.

"Do you want him to come by, Abi?" she persisted.

"Fine," I said. Maybe I could persuade him to stay. Better yet, maybe he would take me with him. Mom left for work. She didn't know what time he was going to be coming by. I started packing some clothes and other things to bring with me. I waited.

Finally he came tearing into the house in a tremendous hurry. He had to be at the airport in 15 minutes he said, grabbing things from the closets and throwing them in his suitcase like a madman. He wouldn't look at me.

"No, I can't bring you with me to California. Your mother would murder me."

"Please, Daddy, I'm sorry I said that stuff last night. I don't know why I said that stuff." He pushed passed me into the study and started packing his laptop and grabbing little things from the desk drawer. Finally he turned to face me.

"I don't understand you women," he said. "I thought you were different than your mother. I thought I understood you."

"I am different than her!" I yelled. "I want to go with you!" He walked away from me into the garage to get his precious tools. I ran up to my room and grabbed my suitcase and my pillow. I put them in the rental car and climbed inside. Dad came flying out the door, dropping first his coat and then some books he had under his arm.

Breathe
Take a deep belly breath in through your nose. Pull the air in until you feel your belly expand as far as possible. Hold your breath there for just a moment, and then let it out slowly through your mouth. Repeat 3 or 4 times with a soothing word, like "sweet," or "calm." Concentrate on just your breathing and nothing else.

"Good-bye, Abi," he yelled back toward the house. "I'll call you." I'll never forget the look on his face when he turned and saw me in the car. His red, sweaty face shifted from irritated to truly angry. It made me want to die. He must have seen that in my face.

"Oh, Abi," he sighed, his face softening a little. "I'm sorry. There is just no way." I got out of the car. He took my suitcase and pillow out of the back seat and put them on the ground. I threw my arms around him, but he didn't hug me back. He just patted my shoulder awkwardly, then put his hands behind his back and gently brought my hands in front of him and held them in his. "I'll call you, Abi," he said, looking into my eyes. I couldn't talk.

Chapter 23

Having a Friend Can Help

I went over to Tara's before my mom came home from work. Tara asked me why I hadn't been at school.

"Can I tell you down by the river?"

She looked at me. "Sure, let me give Bear some food and then we'll go." She didn't say anything about how I looked, which was nice of her. I hadn't done anything with my hair, and I knew my eyes were swollen from crying. All the way down to the river path she didn't say anything and I didn't say anything, but it was comforting to be with her.

"My parents are separating and it's all because I opened my big mouth."

"What do you mean?"

I told her the whole story. The boundaries group, me getting worried my dad was sexually abusing me, the hotline counselor, thinking I should stick up for myself, my parents fighting, and my dad leaving.

"Does he think it's your fault?"

"No. Yes. I don't know. He says I'm being brainwashed by all the

Be Patient

Remember that feelings move and change and you won't always feel this way. Imagine the tide, coming in and going out. Your feelings and urges are like the waves, and you are like a surfer. Imagine yourself riding the waves. Urge surf. Even strong emotions and urges will relax back into smaller waves of feeling over time.

Taking It All Back

Sometimes when kids tell about abuse, they get scared or confused, or just plain freaked out. Other times, the person or people that the child tells blames them, or gets angry, or tells them that they must be lying.

Sometimes parents want kids to "take it back" because they can't believe the abuse happened, or because they get scared and freaked out too. When this happens, kids sometimes do "take it back," and say that they made the whole thing up, or that they were lying, or trying to get back at the person that they said abused them.

If you have done this, it is important to know that you are not alone. It's also important to know that while telling the truth again might be hard, when you're ready, it's good to try again.

Tara said that after she told her cousin Theresa about what James was doing and Theresa told her mother and her mother told Tara's mother and her brother had to move out, she wanted to call those words back ... a thousand times over. But she said she was never sorry that the abuse stopped. Abi

therapy stuff. I think I hurt his feelings really bad. I wanted to go to California with him, but he wouldn't let me."

"If he thinks therapy is so bad for you, I don't see why he didn't just take you with him."

I started crying again.

I felt Tara's arms around me. Bear started jumping up against our legs and barking. I tried to kick him away a little without Tara noticing. "I don't see how you could have caused all that, Abi. They must not have been getting along, anyway."

"But don't you see, if I hadn't done that thing with Phil, then none of this would have happened. I never would have thought about boundaries and all that."

Tara gathered Bear up to her chest. "Maybe not, but that still doesn't mean

Remember the Good in the World
Think about the people you love. Look at the lists you have created.

it's all your fault. They probably would have broken up anyway, before too long. It doesn't sound like they were getting along."

"I shouldn't have tried to speak up for myself. I should have kept my big mouth shut. I should have just talked to my dad without my mother there."

Tara sighed. "Wouldah, shouldah, couldah. I know about that. After I told my mom about what James was doing, I was surprised when James ended up at Aunt Leena's. I didn't know our family was going to be split up. I am glad he isn't touching me that way anymore, but nobody has any idea how much I miss him."

"But my father wasn't abusing me! I just thought he might be before I talked to the hotline counselor. I was mixed up. Now my mother probably thinks he was abusing me. I wish I was dead." I hit the trunk of a tree with my fist.

The puppy barked in Tara's arms. Tara put him down. "Let's go talk to my mom. She's probably home by now. She might have an idea."

"I don't even know her."

"She's nice, Abi."

Tara's mom was home, but she was busy helping Sammy with his homework. "I'll just go home," I told Tara.

"No!" she whispered, holding onto my arm. "Mom, can you please talk with me and Abi in my bedroom for a minute? It's important." Her mother looked from Tara to

Reach Out
Call your therapist. Call a friend. Tell an adult you're having a hard time being alone. Ask someone to sit with you when you are having strong feelings.

me and then back to Tara.

"Yes. Let me get Sammy set up here. I'll be right with you." Tara pulled me into her bedroom. She shoved some teddy bears aside to make room for us on her bed.

"I guess this is your collection."

Tara put a worn looking bear with a striped stocking cap in my

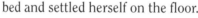

arms. "They keep me company." The door opened and Tara's mom came in. She helped herself to a pillow off the bed and settled herself on the floor.

"What's up girls?"

Tara told her what had happened. About me being afraid my father was abusing me and me calling the child abuse hotline, and then what happened when I talked to my parents. "Now she wants to be dead."

I frowned at Tara.

Her mother shook her head slowly. "Whew."

"She thinks it is all her fault," Tara said.

Her mother made a soft noise in her throat. I looked at her kind face and started to cry again.

My BIG "To Do" List

- Become a community leader.
- Hold a baby lamb.
- Fall in love.
- Bike the Alcan Highway.
- Backpack across Europe.
- Build a house with Habitat for Humanity.
- Sing in front of a crowd.
- Become a Bush pilot.

"It is hard enough just having your parents fight, and it must feel worse to have them separate." She made the soft noise again. "Don't blame yourself, Honey." Tara handed me a roll of toilet paper to blow my nose. I kept crying and blowing my nose. I didn't feel like I had to say anything.

I ended up staying for dinner and playing rummy afterwards with Tara and her little brother and sister. Tara's mom called my mom to see if I could stay for dinner, and later she gave me a ride home. It was after ten when I walked in the front door, but my mom didn't say anything about the time. She hugged me. I was still mad at her, but I let her hug me. She told me we both had an appointment with Jean in the morning to talk about everything.

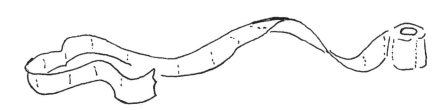

Chapter 24

Therapists Stink

When Jean came out to the waiting room to get us, she smiled at me and said hello. I didn't waste a smile on her. Jean sat in her usual chair. I sat on the little couch next to the table where I like to sit. My mother couldn't decide whether to sit by me or in the rocking chair. Her head went back and forth like a dog watching a game of catch. I tried to ignore her. Finally she chose the chair. Jean had already set some clay out on the table for me. I didn't feel like making anything.

Jean leaned toward me. "Your mother has told me about some big changes that have been going on in your lives, Abi. I'm so sorry your parents are separating." I picked at my sock.

"Many kids blame themselves when their parents have difficulties." Jean said.

"Actually, I think it is her fault. If she'd been nicer to my dad, he wouldn't have ..." I felt sick to my stomach.

"Wouldn't have what, Abi?"

"I don't want to be here," I said.

My mother started crying. Jean handed her a tissue.

"I don't see why I can't go to California with Dad. I don't see why I have to stay here with her. Dad thinks it's all this therapy that's making me weird, anyway. If you hadn't had that stupid hotline brochure in your office this never would have happened."

"Your father and I have been having problems for a long time, Abi, even before we moved to Bluff." My mother blew her nose. "We've talked about separating for years, but we wanted to stay together for your sake."

"I don't want to be here." I said. "I really don't want to be here."

"I'm just saying it wasn't anything you did that made us break up."

"Don't lie to me." I said. My teeth were clamped together, I guess so I wouldn't scream.

Jean had been making little bricks out of the blue clay and standing them one behind another on the table. "You spoke the truth about what was happening in your family, Abi. Sometimes even a tiny bit of truth can make an unstable situation collapse. It didn't take much." Jean touched the brick on the end and the row toppled like dominoes. "It must be very painful for all three of you." My mother blew her nose again.

"I miss my dad," I whispered.

"This doesn't mean you won't be able to see and talk to your dad, Abi," my mother said. "I just want to make sure it is safe and healthy for you."

"He wasn't abusing me!"

Things that Make Me Happy

- ♥ Sweatpants that don't look like sweatpants.
- ♥ Friends I can call at 4 a.m.
- ♥ Dark chocolate.
- ♥ Rolling down hills and getting grass stains on my knees.
- ♥ Shooting corner shots.
- ♥ New socks.
- ♥ Falling snow.
- ♥ Popcorn with lots of butter.
- ♥ Kayaking on a smooth ocean.
- ♥ Olives.
- ♥ Surprises.
- ♥ Birthday parties.
- ♥ Milkshakes.
- ♥ Accomplishing something I never thought I would.

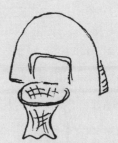

Not all of these are mine. Abi

"It isn't fair for him to treat you like a girlfriend." My mother tried to look interested and concerned. I hated the way her eyes were red and glistening.

I turned toward Jean. "Maybe that was just my imagination. I was all mixed up because of therapy. At least my dad paid attention to me. At least he loved me." Before I screwed things up, I thought to myself.

"He still loves you, Abi. And I love you, too." Mom's voice sounded like she cared about me. I figured that was for Jean's benefit.

"Right," I muttered. "When can I see him?"

"Your parents will be discussing that, Abi." Jean said. "This is a confusing situation. It is no wonder you feel mixed up. I'm sorry your parents are having difficulties. You brought up some very reasonable concerns, but they weren't able to look at them with you and work out a solution together." I was feeling so angry and hopeless it was hard for me to hear what she was saying. "Don't give up, Abi. You have two loving parents who both want you to have what is best for you and I'm committed to helping the three of you work this out."

I didn't talk to my mother on the way home.

Jake called me that night after dinner. I took the phone into my bedroom. He wanted to know why I hadn't been in school on Friday. I told him my parents were splitting up and I was depressed. He didn't make fun of me. His parents have been divorced for three years.

"I hated it when my dad left. I was so pissed off. I hated my dad and I hated his girlfriend and I hated my mom for letting it happen."

"Are you still mad at them?"

"Not all the time. When I see other kids' parents at their games or things like that, I think, why can't my parents still be together? But most of the time it's okay." He paused. "The thing is I didn't really realize there was any problem. It's not like they were fighting all the time. It was a shock."

When Parents Get in Your Space

"Emotional incest" describes what happens when a parent doesn't create boundaries with their child. Parents are supposed to set rules, guidelines, and consequences for their children. They may enjoy spending time with their children, and have lots of fun together, but parents are not supposed to be their child's buddy. Kids can make lots of different kinds of friends, but they need their parents to be parents.

When parents lean on their children to meet their own emotional needs, make them into friends, or share too much adult information with them, children can't keep their boundaries. Part of you might like the special status that being your parent's friend and knowing adult information gets you. Another part might feel confused, sad, and angry. Usually you don't even know why.

Parents who are using "emotional incest" to meet their own needs may give their children the message that the children's friends or boyfriends are never "good enough." They may treat their child like an adult friend, sharing secrets with her or asking her advice about their love life or about other adult decisions, like finances. They may have few or no boundaries with their children, going into their child's personal space, looking through their child's things, getting involved in their child's decisions or with her friends.

When these things happen, it is very hard for children to feel like they are their own person with their own rights and thoughts and feelings. A child may feel responsible for her parent's feelings or happiness. She may feel like she has to give up her own interests, activities, or feelings in order to take care of a parent. These are not things kids should have to do!

If you feel any of these things, it may help to talk to someone outside of your family about it.[1]

My dad should have read this. Abi

I found myself nodding into the phone. "I guess I should have known my parents were thinking of splitting up. They had a lot of arguments. And they never touched each other, never hugged or kissed. But I was clueless."

"This is the worst time, Abi. Then you gradually get used to it." It was a nice thing to say, but I didn't believe him.

Jake asked me to go swimming with him on Sunday. I said yes, but I didn't really feel like going. The movies had been fun; it wasn't that, I just didn't feel like doing anything.

My mom slipped an envelope under my door.

I read the note through three times. Then I tore it into tiny pieces and put them in a pile outside my door. I locked my door. It was weird. When I was around my mother I couldn't help hating her and blaming her for my father leaving. When I was by myself or with Tara and her mom I blamed myself and my stupid guardian angel, though I wondered if I even had one. When I was with Jean I blamed her and the hotline counselor. When my dad was leaving I felt like it was all his fault. I was mad at everyone.

Dear Abigail,

I realize that I have been distant from you and your father. That has been harmful to you. I don't just blame your father for all this mess. I blame myself, too. I've been worried about Grandma, and what was happening at home took the back burner for me. That needs to change. Hopefully, you and I can work together to have a closer relationship. Also, I want you to know that I will do what I can to help you have a healthy relationship with your father. I am not trying to take him away from you. I love you.

Mom

Chapter 25

More Hard Things Happen to Tara and Me

Sunday afternoon, Jake and I went to the pool during Open Swim. We walked together from my house. Some other kids from school were swimming and we played Keep-Away for a while. It was girls against boys. Whenever I had the ball Jake was all over me. I have to admit that when he had the ball I was the same way. I grabbed his ankle and pulled myself up his leg to try to get to his arm, but before I could get there he threw the ball to another guy. I screamed and tried to swim toward the ball but he wrapped his arms around my waist. Finally I wriggled free. It was exciting to slide against him. I felt like a dolphin or a mermaid. Everyone was yelling and laughing. We played until Amy and Shannon quit and went over to the diving board.

Jake reached over and took my hand. "You're stunning."

All the laughter drained out of me. Those were Phil's exact words. I felt like puking.

"Hey," Jake said looking worried. "Relax. It's no big deal. I'm sorry I brought it up. I'll race you across the pool."

"I've got to go." I climbed out and walked to the locker room without looking back. I took a quick shower and got dressed before any of the other girls got out. Jake must have stayed in the pool. Thank God.

When I got home, Mom was packing boxes. I felt a surge of relief. "We're going back to California!" I threw my coat off and started dancing around. Mom sagged into a chair and watched me with a pained look on her face.

"Abi." She sighed. "We're moving in with your grandmother."

"You've got to be kidding! She hates me." Mom just stared at me stubbornly. I ran up to my room and slammed the door.

Anger and Your Body

When you are angry, your whole body goes into "fight, flight or freeze" mode. Your brain might kick into fighting mode, which means you will fight with words or actions. It might push you to run away or to get out of the situation in any way that you can. Or, it might 'freeze' and leave you unable to get out of the situation or to say or do anything to help yourself. This is the same brain and body system that is activated when a person is abused. That means that, for some people, when they are angry, their body and brain are triggered to remember the abuse, or, when they think about the abuse, their body and brain are triggered into becoming automatically angry. One way to tell whether your angry reaction is about what is going on now or is an automatic reaction based on your abuse experience is proportion. Ask yourself, "Is what's going on now worth this big a reaction? Is there something about what is happening now that reminds me of the abuse?"

I didn't talk to my mother until the next morning. She wanted me to go to school. I was buried under my covers, but I felt like I was buried under a thick sludge of dread.

"I'm sick," I moaned.

"If you were well enough to go swimming yesterday, you're well enough to go to school today." I didn't get up. She knocked on my door a few more times and made threats about me not getting to see Jake or my other friends. If only she knew. Jake was exactly who I didn't want to see. Finally she gave up. I pulled the covers over my head. I must have fallen asleep because the next time she knocked it was in my dream.

"Go away," my dream self said. The knocking continued. I opened my eyes.

"It's me, Tara. I want to talk to you." Tara! Why wasn't she in school? Maybe I was still dreaming. I was surprised my mother had let her come up.

How Do You Feel about Your Body?

Do you like your body? Are you comfortable with the sensations in your breasts and genitals when you think about sexy things or touch yourself? Sexual sensations can be intense. It is important to give yourself time to gradually get used to them, perhaps by touching yourself. After some types of sexual abuse, you may need to learn to enjoy sexual sensations. A counselor can talk with you about this and help you heal, but a counselor should never touch you sexually. That would be sexual abuse.[1]

"Just a minute." I sat up and looked at the clock. Four-thirty. I had slept all day. I dragged myself out of bed, combed my hair with my fingers, and opened the door. After all that sleep I still felt groggy.

Tara looked worried. "What's up? Are you really sick?"

I sighed. "I don't know. I slept all day and I still feel tired. And I'm really thirsty. I can't believe my mom let you come up and see me."

"She said it might do you good to talk to a friend."

"She did?"

"Yeah, why wouldn't she?"

I shrugged. "I don't know." Tara stilled looked worried or something. Her eyes were reddish, like she had been crying or had allergies.

"Do you want something to drink?" I asked. As we went down to the kitchen I noticed my mother packing boxes in the living room. I frowned at her. We brought some apple juice up to my room.

THE THURSDAY GROUP: A Story and Information for Girls Healing from Sexual Abuse

"What about you?" I asked. I didn't feel like talking about what happened with Jake. "Are you okay?"

Tara picked up a little pillow off of my bed and hugged it against her stomach. She made a face. "Not really."

She had found out from her cousin Theresa that their Uncle Leroy had sexually abused James.

"That's horrible. Is that who James is staying with now?"

"No. He's staying with Aunt Leena and Uncle Frank. But Theresa said that a few years ago Uncle Leroy abused her and James." Tears were running down Tara's cheeks. I jumped up and got her some toilet paper from the bathroom. She blew her nose. I didn't know what to say.

Tara was clutching the pillow like a flotation device. "He knew what it felt like to be abused and he still abused me," she whispered. "I hate him."

"No wonder you feel bad," I said. "Does your mother know?"

"Everybody knows I'm mad at him," she mumbled.

Relationships & Sexuality

Dealing with sexual feelings, being close to and trusting other people after you have been abused can be tricky.

It's common for people to get stuck in extremes:

Either being too trusting and open with everyone they meet, even telling strangers about the abuse, or going alone with people who aren't safe.

Or, the opposite: having difficulty trusting, talking to, and staying close to even the very nicest, warmest, and most loving and trustworthy of people.

"No, I mean, does she know your uncle abused James?"

Tara looked at me, her mouth dropped open. "I don't know ... maybe not. Maybe Mom doesn't know about it." She thought for a moment. "I need to ask her. Will you come with me?"

"Yeah," I said, then, "if my mother will let me."

First she wanted us to eat dinner. Then she wanted Tara to help me with the homework I had missed. Finally she said I could go if I swore to her I would go to school on Tuesday, no matter how I felt in the morning. I thought about Jake and almost said no. Then I looked at Tara.

"I promise." I said, holding up my hands to show my fingers weren't crossed the way I used to do when I was little.

"Home by 9:45, Abi," she said, almost smiling.

Tara's mother was saying good night to Melissa and Sammy when we got to their house. We made ourselves some hot chocolate while we waited for her.

"Do you want some hot chocolate, Mom?" Tara asked, when her mother came into the kitchen. "The water is still hot."

> ### Imagine Holding Hands — How do You Feel Before, During, After?
> You might feel happy, excited, loved, scared, ashamed, confused, or any combination of these. Make a list of different situations (walking side-by-side, holding hands, talking about feelings, sharing strong emotions, kissing, having someone you like a lot touch your breasts, nudity, sexual intercourse, etc.) and write how you have felt or think you might feel before, during and after.[2]

"I'd love some." She smiled at us and sank into a chair. I was surprised at how quiet Tara's face was. I wondered if she would bring up her Uncle or not. I sat down at the table across from her mom. Tara brought her mother's hot chocolate to the table and sat down next to me. Nobody said anything. I wondered if Tara wanted me to bring it up. She was staring down at her hot chocolate, so I couldn't catch her eye.

"Theresa told me something about James," Tara said, still looking down.

Her mom took a sip from her mug. "You want to talk about it, Honey?" Tara sat there without speaking or moving until I couldn't stand it anymore. I patted her arm.

"You said you wanted to ask her."

Tara sighed, then blurted, "Theresa said your brother Leroy abused her and James. I want to know if you knew about it." A cloud of sadness moved across her mom's face, making her look about ten years older. She nodded.

"Why didn't you tell me?" Tara asked.

"It happened quite a few years ago, Tara. James and your cousin were only ten when we found out. That means you were only five. Then Leroy moved to Anchorage and we didn't see much of him. I don't know why I didn't tell you. We just never talked about it. It never seemed to come up. I would have warned you if he were still living around here."

"Did Uncle Leroy go to jail?"

Tara's mom shook her head slowly. "We never told the police." I wanted to ask why, but I held my tongue.

She kept talking in a slow, tired voice. "We didn't want James and Theresa to have to talk to strangers

> **Myth:** People who offend are sexually frustrated or aren't able to have sex with someone their own age.
> **Fact:** Having sex with appropriate same-aged partners does not stop people from offending. People who offend against children do so because they are interested in being sexual with children.

about it or be in a trial. I guess I was afraid somebody might take James away from us because we let it happen. Leena and I just wanted Leroy to leave and never come back." She kneaded her forehead with her fingers. "We handled it ourselves. Your father and your Uncle Frank went out to Leroy's place and told him that there was no room for him in Bluff anymore. He moved to Anchorage the next week." I noticed some tears starting to come out of her eyes, and looked away. "Oh Tara, I keep thinking that if only we had gotten some counseling for James then maybe he wouldn't have hurt you."

"I don't understand," Tara said. "Why would being abused make you want to abuse someone else?"

"I don't know. Most people don't react that way, but some do. It is as if they are trying to get control of the confusing feelings," Tara's mom said. "I'm just learning about it myself. I'm finally getting counseling for when Leroy and I were abused by our father."

"Grandpa!"

"Yes, Tara."

I couldn't believe it. Poor Tara. Finding out about so much abuse in her family.

She stood up, clutching her arms around herself as if she was cold. Her face was ashen. "Why didn't you tell me? Why didn't anybody tell me? If I had known about all this maybe I would have been able to stop it. Or ask for help sooner!"

Myth: Sexual abuse is a cultural norm in some Alaska Native villages.
Fact: Child sexual abuse was never considered normal or appropriate in Native communities. Sexual abuse of children had severe consequences before Native American and Alaska Native people experienced contact with non-Native people. In many villages abusers were shunned, threatened, isolated, or even banished or killed. People who were abused were often brought to a traditional healer for ceremony and healing. Restitution to the victim and the family of the victim was expected. Before the historical traumas of widespread epidemics and mass kidnapping of children into boarding schools, child sexual abuse was uncommon and children and women were honored. Men were respected and valued.

Reasons People Don't Tell about Sexual Abuse

- Fears that the results of telling will be worse than the abuse.
- Belief that they did something wrong or that they will get in trouble.
- Embarrassment about having to talk about sexual things, especially to a stranger.
- Fears that they caused the abuse, or did nothing to stop it.
- Fears that there is something wrong with them.
- Fears about being disloyal or hurtful to the family.
- Fears about the strength of their own anger or temper.
- Not seeing the abuse as abusive.
- Not remembering or not wanting to think about the abuse.
- Fears about not knowing what to say when they are asked questions.
- Fears that no one will believe them.
- Fears about being removed from their home or from the people who care for them.
- Fears that the abuser will follow through with threats to hurt them or their family members.
- Fears about having to see the person who abused them.
- Fears about having to go to court.
- Shame that they didn't tell somebody the first time it happened.
- Their feelings of love or respect for the person who is abusing them.

I felt weird sitting there looking up at her, so I stood up and put my arms around her. She was shaking. I felt so bad for her and her mom. The tears were pouring down her mother's face.

"I'm so sorry, Honey. I'm just so sorry. You're right, I should've told you."

I could feel Tara clenching and unclenching her fists. Tara's mom's face was twisted in pain. I didn't know what to do.

"Honey, it's the hardest thing in the world to talk about. But I should've told you. You have a right to be angry with me." As soon as she said that, Tara started sobbing. Her mom got up and put her arms around both of us. I was crying too. I couldn't help it. I didn't know if my tears were for them or for me.

Cycles of Abuse (Intergenerational Patterns)

Sexual abuse sometimes happens in patterns among family members. When this occurs, it is called intergenerational abuse, because it happens across generations. Abuse happens in cycles like this for two main reasons.

The first occurs when people in the family really don't know that sexual abuse is wrong and doesn't normally happen in other families (this is very rare, but it does happen). The second is when the people who have been abused don't get help to understand their feelings, and so they try to get rid of their negative feelings by abusing someone else.

Most people who have been sexually abused never abuse anyone else. But sometimes, when a person doesn't take care of their big feelings about the abuse, or about other things that have happened in their lives, it can build up inside until that person starts to abuse someone else.

It is important to look at the types of patterns that occur in your family, not just patterns about abuse, but patterns of positive things as well. When you understand your family patterns, you have more control over whether you want to follow the family pattern or do something different.

I sure hope I don't turn out like my mother. Abi

Chapter 26

Getting Our Buttons Pushed

The next few days of school went by in a blur. I talked to Jake, but only about easy things, not how I was feeling on the inside. I acted like I was fine.

It was a relief to walk into the group room on Thursday afternoon. I felt like I could breathe again. Finally I could get a break from working so hard to act normal when my whole world was falling apart.

I had a hard time hearing what the others were saying during the talking circle check in. I was trying to figure out what to say. When Tara handed me the stone I rubbed the familiar shape with my fingers. So much had happened since the last group. I remembered Carol telling us to speak up for ourselves, and felt a wave of anger. I pictured my dad leaving. I didn't feel like going into all that.

"Jake told me I was stunning when we were swimming, and it made me feel like throwing up." I said, finally. "It was the same thing Phil told me when he was taking those pictures."

"It sounds like Jake's words triggered a physical response in your body," Carol said.

Danielle started bouncing on the couch. "I get triggered all the time. I get flashbacks. That's what I'm doing the EMDR for."

I was totally confused. "I don't have a clue about what either of you are talking about."

Carol smiled reassuringly. "I guess we are talking about several different things here, but they are connected. A flashback is one type of automatic response, but it isn't the only kind. It's pretty common for people's buttons to get pushed by words, smells, colors, all kinds of things, really. Maybe Danielle could tell us what she means by flashbacks and then we could talk about how feelings and memories from the past can get triggered by things in the present. Are you okay with that, Abi?" I nodded.

Danielle started twisting one of her ringlets around her finger. "A flashback is when something reminds you of what happened and you feel almost like it's happening again. Last week I was in the mall with my friend, Lacy, and all of a sudden she grabs my wrist because she sees a boy she likes. I yanked my arm away from her and ran into the bathroom. It was horrible. She came in to find me and I was hiding in one of the stalls. I was so embarrassed." Danielle's freckles were standing out from her face again.

"Was it the boy that scared you?" Tara asked.

"No, it was when Lacy grabbed my wrist. It reminded me of when I was trying to get away and that guy grabbed my wrist."

Tara reached over and held her hand next to Danielle's, palm up, like a question. Danielle took Tara's hand. "Thanks," she said. She scooted closer to Tara on the couch. "Anyway, the EMDR is supposed to help with not having so many flashbacks."

"Thanks, Danielle," Carol said. "That was a

Coping with Difficult Memories, Big Feelings, or Flashbacks

If you have a bad memory that keeps pushing into your mind, and you can't get rid of it, here is something you can try which may help take intensity or power away from the memory.

Try adding something funny or weird to the memory. For example, if you are remembering an abuse incident, you might imagine a tidal wave of friendly polka dotted hippopotamuses flowing in between you and the abuser and carrying you away to safety.

You can imagine the picture, or even draw or paint it. Sometimes creating bizarre visual images can help take power away from pushy memories.

great example. Memories are stored not just in our brains, but also in our bodies. Memories of an extremely disturbing event can get stored in a tangled memory ball. In the ball are the emotions, physical sensations, and thoughts we were having during the event. When something happens that reminds us of any of those tangled memories, the feelings, thoughts, and sensations from the event can come flooding back. It could be a sound or a smell or a touch, anything, really can push the button and trigger a response in our bodies. It can feel like the event is happening all over again, and you may not know that you are in the present and safe." Carol paused.

"A flashback is one type of automatic sensory response, but not the only kind." She looked at me. "You felt a wave of nausea triggered by Jake's words, Abigail, but it wasn't a flashback because you didn't relive the abusive event. In addition to nausea, sometimes survivors of abuse experience waves of anger, fear, or numbness in response to sensory triggers. Often people have no idea what in the world has suddenly made them feel so upset."

"That happens to me and it makes me feel crazy!" Imaya blurted. Carol smiled.

> ### Remember Your Safe Place
> Make it as real as possible by imagining what it would feel like to be there: sounds you might hear there; any sensations such as warmth, wind or water; any smells. Some people can see their safe place clearly in their mind's eye; other people have more of a feeling of being there, or a sense of imagining it. However you do it is fine.

"I know what you mean, Imaya, but it is completely normal. The good news is that there are lots of things we can do that will help untangle the simple memory of a hurtful event from the flood of connected feelings and body sensations. Desensitization therapies, like the EMDR that Danielle is doing, are just one example."

She made it sound like she had automatic responses, too. I was still mixed up about what happened in the pool, because, actually, when Phil had told me I looked stunning, it felt kind of nice. I knew the clothes were not anything my mom would let me wear, and the way he was having me pose was like something from a movie. It made me feel daring and grown-up, and only a little nervous. It was more afterwards when I found out it was sexual abuse that I got so confused and ashamed. Maybe all of that was the bad memory, not just what Phil did, but everything that happened afterwards, too. It seemed like anytime anybody thought my body looked nice, I was afraid it was something bad, something bad about them and something bad about me.

"It is almost like there is a watchdog part of our brain," Carol was saying. "It watches out for anything that reminds you of the hurtful event and sounds the alarm inside your body. If someone tells Abi how beautiful she is, instead of feeling nice, she feels confused and anxious, because of the alarm system going off inside her body.

"Anytime we are having strong, uncomfortable feelings, there are things we can do to help ourselves," Carol said. "We've talked about this before."

"What I hate," Jessica blurted, "is how you are feeling okay and then all of a sudden, out of the blue, the bad feelings take over. You don't have any warning and then suddenly you feel like you've been run over. I don't have time to think about the list we made." I knew exactly what she meant.

"It's hard to think when a truckload of difficult feelings have just slammed into you," Carol said, slamming her fist into her hand. Imaya and Danielle jumped.

"I'm so sorry," Carol exclaimed. "I didn't mean to startle you." Imaya started giggling, then Danielle, and pretty soon all of us were.

"That pushed my buttons!" Imaya said, smiling.

"I want you to try using a short list any time you are having an automatic response or a flood of uncomfortable feelings," Carol said. "A list so short you won't need to write it down. Ready?" We nodded. She held up one finger. "Name it." She held up two fingers. "Breathe." She held up three fingers. "Be a friend to yourself." We must have looked confused, because she laughed. "Let's take a stretch break and then I'll explain.

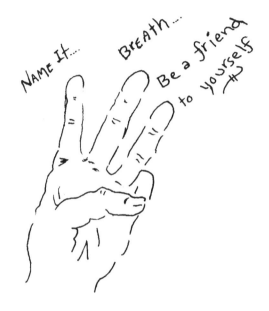

Chapter 27

The Short List

"Okay, let me explain. You want to name what is happening. Tell yourself: 'This is an automatic response,' or 'These are feelings from the past,' or 'I feel scared.' Putting your feelings into words makes them less overwhelming. Then take a deep belly breath and let it out very slowly. You can count to five, hiss, or use a calming word. A few slow belly breaths will help you relax and help your body feel better." She demonstrated a slow belly breath.

"And be your own friend. Don't start getting mad at yourself for feeling upset. In your imagination reach out your hand to yourself the way Tara did to Danielle. Be a friend to yourself. Ask yourself what you need and try to get that for yourself. Maybe you need some comforting words, someone to give you a hug, or a drink of water, something off the longer list we made. You may need to go to your safe place or use your Comfort Box. Actions that help your body reconnect to what is around you in the present, like drinking water or talking to someone, are great. Maybe you need to find out some more information. Telling yourself there is something wrong with you for feeling the way you are feeling only makes things worse. So..." She looked at us expectantly.

"Be a friend to yourself," Danielle and I chorused. Carol smiled. "I want this list to stick in your mind. Let's all say it out loud a few times." Imaya and I rolled our eyes at each other.

We started chanting. "NAME IT * BREATHE * BE A FRIEND TO YOURSELF. NAME IT * BREATHE * BE A FRIEND TO YOURSELF. NAME IT * BREATHE * BE A FRIEND TO YOURSELF." Imaya stood up and started clapping slowly in time to the chant. Tara and Danielle and I stood up too, and we started marching around the room. Chanting louder and louder. Jessica and Carol clapped along. "NAME IT * BREATHE * BE A FRIEND TO YOURSELF. NAME IT * BREATHE * BE A FRIEND TO YOURSELF."

I wondered if that would have helped me in the pool. I still felt so confused about all that stuff. Carol must have been reading my mind.

"Do you think the short list would have helped you, Abi, when you felt like vomiting after Jake said you were beautiful?" she asked me after we had all sat down.

"I could have said to myself, I feel sick, and I could have breathed." Then I mumbled, "I don't think I could have been very friendly to myself." Imaya reached her hand out toward me, the way Tara had to Danielle. I sat there with my hands in my lap, feeling embarrassed. Imaya pulled her hand back.

"Kids who have been sexually abused often blame themselves for normal feelings," Carol said, and added gently, "It doesn't look like you are being very friendly toward yourself right now."

That made me mad. "I hate you. I hate this group! It doesn't help me at all. Last time you wanted us to stick up for ourselves, so I did, and now my parents are getting a divorce. I can't be a friend to myself. That's the stupidest thing I've ever heard. My dad was right. This group is bad for me." I scrambled up out of the beanbag chair and headed for the door. As I was leaving I heard Carol saying quietly,

"What a week. Anyone would be upset."

> **Myth:** **After you heal you won't have any more automatic responses.**
>
> **Fact:** Healing means that you will have fewer automatic responses, and when you do have them, you will be able to comfort and support yourself, and/or ask for the support you need from others. You will still have automatic responses. We all have them. But you will learn to control them, rather than the other way 'round.

As soon as I got to the waiting room, I wished I hadn't left. A woman and her two little children were staring at me. I went out the front doors, but regretted that, too. The pussy willows on the bushes outside the door whipped wildly in the wind. I'd left my jacket in the group room. Tara came out.

"It's cold out here," she said.

"I made a fool out of myself," I whispered, shivering.

"Everybody understands. Give yourself a break."

"Yeah, yeah, I know," I said with a half smile, "Be a friend to yourself."

Tara laughed. She put her arm through mine. "Come on back inside, okay?" When we got back to the group room, I was relieved to see everyone busy looking through magazines and cutting out pictures.

Be a Better Friend to Yourself

Repeat affirmations or calming words.

- ☼ I am a good and kind person.
- ☼ I deserve to be loved.
- ☼ I am learning every day.
- ☼ I am whole and sacred.
- ☼ I can handle this.
- ☼ I am worthwhile.
- ☼ I am lovable.
- ☼ I can ask for help.
- ☼ I am learning to let others in.
- ☼ I am learning to trust others.
- ☼ I am learning to trust myself.
- ☼ I am loving.
- ☼ I can enjoy the company of others.

Carol looked at us and smiled. "I'm glad you are back."

"Me, too," Danielle said, and the other girls nodded. I felt exhausted.

Carol handed us some blank paper. "We are making collages. You can choose a topic, but it should be something about yourself. For example, things that are important to you, things you like, things you hate, or things you would like in your life. Cutting and gluing the images onto your own paper can help you work through feelings. Or the collage may help remind you of your goals." I didn't want to think about anything or make any decisions, so I just started looking through the magazines.

It was quiet for a while. I started to let the peacefulness of the room and my friends seep into me. I decided to make a collage about things I like, because I found a picture of a piano and one of a river. I thought I might paste them next to each other, because I want to play a duet with a river some day.

Carol's voice startled me. "I wish I could promise each of you that when you speak up for yourselves others will listen and respect you. I'm afraid that isn't what always happens. I wish we had talked about that more last time. We can't always predict how someone else will respond."

"I didn't know my family would fall apart," I whispered.

"I'm so sorry," Carol said. "How very painful for you." She handed me the glue stick, which I had been hunting around for. "Abi, no matter what you said, you didn't cause your parent's marriage to fall apart."

"That's what my therapist said, too."

"I'm glad you are talking about this with your therapist. You deserve help and support with this."

"Okay." I said. I didn't want to talk about it anymore.

Chapter 28
. . . .
The Forest Fire

When we pulled out onto the main road we saw a huge gray cloud of smoke coming up from near where Grandma lives. "We'd better go check on her," Mom said, pulling into a side road and turning around. She switched on the radio.

"There is a forest fire burning out of control near the Aspen Subdivision on the west side of town. The police are advising everyone who can see and smell the smoke to evacuate their homes. The wind is blowing the fire northwest toward the river and the residential area. Volunteer firefighters are on the scene and a crew of smoke jumpers is responding from Anchorage. Please stay out of the area." Mom looked grim.

"Is Grandma's subdivision Aspen?" I asked. Mom shook her head.

"No, Cottonwood, but that's just on the other side of Aspen." Up ahead a cop was standing next to a parked police car stopping the cars. The truck in front of us did a U turn and headed back the other direction after the driver talked to him. We pulled up and Mom rolled her window down.

"We're asking people to stay out of the area of the fire," he said.

"I need to get to my mother in Cottonwood subdivision. She can't drive and will need help to get out of the house. She is all alone." Mom was determined. He didn't argue, but waved us right through.

Grandma was sleeping when we got there. She didn't even know about the fire. Mom switched on the radio in the house. I went out in the yard. I couldn't see the smoke because of the trees around the house. I didn't smell any smoke. The man next door was watering his lawn. It seemed like an odd thing to be doing at a time like this.

"You should get a hose out and water around your grandma's house," he called to me. "It may help keep it from burning." I found a hose in the garage and started spraying. It was good to have something to do, but I wished I were helping fight the fire. I wanted to go inside to listen to the radio reports. I wished my dad were there. Grandma's neighbor finished on his lawn and started spraying his house. Mike from my math class, a guy I thought might be interested in me, rode up on his bicycle with what looked like a bunch of dirty brown towels under his arm.

"I'm going to fight the fire!" He tried to look serious, but I could tell he was thrilled.

"I want to come, but my bike's at home."

"I could ride you on my carrying rack."

"You could?"

"Sure, I give my sister rides all the time." I looked toward the house. I figured Mom would probably say no if I asked her. I propped the hose on the fence so it would spray near the house.

Do People Create Their Own Destiny?

Some people believe that you can shape your world through thoughts and feelings.

In many ways, positive thinking (such as, "I deserve good things" or "It's okay to make mistakes as long as I keep trying") can open up options that you would never have known otherwise. And negative thinking (such as, "I'm bad," or "Nobody will ever like me") can make things harder so that you will miss opportunities and not even know that they have passed you by. But any negative thinking you may have done in the past cannot and did not cause you to be abused.

While positive thinking may be very powerful, it cannot change the fact that there are other people in the world who have their own thoughts, feelings, and beliefs that will differ from yours.

Choices made by your ancestors, your community, even your government also limit the ability you have to take complete control over your own life.

"Okay." I swung my leg over the rack and sat down. I wished I wasn't wearing my white painter pants. He handed me the brown things. They were wet burlap bags. I lifted up my feet and Mike stood up on the pedals to get us going. As we rode off the neighbor was yelling something about my mother.

"I'm going to help fight the fire," I yelled to him without looking back.

It wasn't far to the edge of the fire, maybe ten or fifteen blocks if we had been in California. There weren't real blocks in these subdivisions, just curvy dirt roads with houses in among the trees every now and then. Mike left his bike on the road and we ran up to where the other people were. The road we were on made a Y with another road and the fire was coming toward us in the fork of the Y. It was hard to see what was happening because of the smoke. The flames ran along the ground in the dry grass and bushes. The edge of the fire came to a tree and huge flames went shooting up toward the sky, then another tree went up in flames. I gasped.

Things You Can Control

While you cannot completely create your own destiny through the power of thought or feelings, you can make a choice to accept yourself or blame and shame yourself. One will allow you to move and grow and have opportunities and to make your own choices. The other will create more feelings, thoughts, and beliefs about shame and blame, and that will lead to negative behaviors and to missed opportunities. You cannot change what happened to you. And you did not cause or create the abuse that happened to you. But you can make a choice about how to deal with it now.

"We have to beat out any flames that come across the road," Mike said, taking one of the wet sacks from me.

"Have you done this before?" I asked.

"There was a fire in my neighborhood last spring. That's where I learned how." A burning branch blew across the road and landed in the dry grass by his feet. He swung the burlap sack over his head with both hands and then down on the grass. Flames started up on his right. When he started beating that, the first spot burst into flames again. I whacked it with my sack, and then stomped on the sack for good measure. People all around us were using sacks and shovels to put out the little fires. A gust of wind brought more smoke, and the little glowing sticks and dead leaves that were trying to carry the fire forward. The school counselor strode by wearing a fire fighters outfit. He was almost past us before he recognized us.

"You guys be careful, now." He looked like he wanted to say more but he was in too much of a hurry. All I could think about was putting the little fires out. Even though it was horrible in a way, with the fire huge and powerful, in another way it was wonderful, everyone working together to try to stop it. I was a part of it all.

I don't know how long we were working like that before my mom came up behind me. Her face was pale.

"Thank God I found you, Abi! Why didn't you tell me where you were going?"

"I'm sorry. I thought the man next door would tell you."

"Come with me now, Abi. Your grandmother is in the car and I need to get her out of here. She can't breathe because of the smoke."

A burning spruce branch landed next to her and she stepped away from it. I whacked it out with my bag.

"Mom, I've got to stay here and help. Please." She looked angry. I tried to stay calm. "If we have enough people here, maybe we can keep the fire from getting to Grandma's and the other people's houses."

"If the fire gets away from you, you could get hurt."

"It's okay, Mrs. Barnes, I'll make sure she's okay. I've done this before," Mike said. Mom glanced toward Mike and then glared back at me.

"No, Abi. You come NOW." I couldn't believe she was making me come. Mike looked sympathetic.

"Just leave the sack by the water truck." he said. Mom headed back to the car walking very fast, and I ran to catch up with her after I had dropped off the burlap sack. When we got into the car Grandma didn't say anything. Nobody did. I could hear Grandma's breathing. Even though I had been running, she was breathing faster than I was. I felt miserable. I knew I should have told Mom where I was going, but then she wouldn't have let me come. Why hadn't she just rescued Grandma? I didn't need rescuing.

At home I helped Mom get Grandma settled on the couch. Her breathing was quieter.

"Play something for me, Abi," my grandma whispered. I hugged her.

"Sure, Grandma." While I was playing I kept thinking about Mike.

After Grandma fell asleep, I went into the kitchen. My mom had the radio on.

"The fire is under control." She said, with a dead sounding voice. The way she used to talk to my dad.

"Yes!" I cheered. "How did they stop it?" Ignoring her deadness.

"Planes dropping fire retardant helped." I hate it when she's like that. I wanted to scream at her, make her yell, cry, anything.

"Mom," I said, "why don't you just yell at me?" She looked at me with her empty face and just barely shook her head no.

"I could have lost you both," she whispered.

"Mom!" I started to raise my voice but remembered Grandma. "I was okay. There were lots of people there helping. There was a water truck." She crossed her arms on the table and put her head down.

"I'm sorry," I said quickly. I ran up to my room.

Part of me wasn't sorry at all.

Chapter 29

. . . .

Being a Friend to Myself

The next day my father called. I heard my mother talking on the phone to someone for a long time, and then she called me to pick up the phone. I was surprised when she said it was him because they never used to talk that much when he was home. He told me he loved me and it wasn't my fault he and Mom were separated. When I started crying he changed the subject and started talking about a movie he had seen

What Can Kids Do to Help Deal with Abuse?
Get involved! Join an activist group that works to end abuse and help people heal in the process. Making meaning out of your own pain by helping someone else can feel very powerful and be healing all at the same time.

that he thought I would like. I'd already seen it, but I didn't really feel like talking about it. My throat was sore from needing to cry. He said something about not knowing how to talk to me anymore.

"I miss you, Daddy," I said. Then I really started to cry.

"Don't cry, Honey. I miss you, too," he said.

I couldn't say anything else because I was crying.

"Be careful now, Kiddo, you're going to flood the connection there." That made me laugh a little. He wanted to know how it was going with the piece I was learning for a piano recital. We talked about that for a while and then he said he'd call me again.

Myth: After you heal you won't ever think about the abuse.

Fact: Healing has to do with finding things to balance out the abuse. The love and caring of others can help balance the awfulness of the abuse. Other things can help, like watching a flock of sandpipers turn all at once and flash the sun on their wings, or laughing with friends until your face aches. When you do think about the abuse, it won't be as distressing. It will have less power to disturb you. You will have more control over when and where you think about the abuse. As you heal in this way, you take your power back from the abuser. You own your healing. Remember, living well and being happy is the best revenge!

After we hung up I cried some more. We hadn't even talked about the fire. He seemed so far away. I felt like dying. I remembered the short list from group. Name it, breathe, be a friend to yourself. Okay, I thought, I'm feeling sad and hopeless. I took a belly breath in through my nose and let it hiss out slowly. I did it again. And again. That felt good. How could I be a friend to myself? Everything I did and everything I felt was wrong.

Suddenly I pictured Tara and me down by the river laughing about how easy it was for each of us to see that the other one's abuse wasn't her fault. I remembered Tara shivering when she came out to get me when I ran out of the group. If I were a friend to myself, I'd be able to see that all of this wasn't my fault. If I were a friend to myself, I might ask if I wanted to go downstairs and play the piano for a while. I took another belly breath and let it hiss out. I got up off my bed and made myself walk down to the piano. First "Für Elise" by Beethoven, very slow and sad. Then I played the "Phantom of the Opera Prelude," pounding the keys. Then I was tired, so I just played "The Snowman" by George Winston, because it was peaceful and I knew it really well.

When I finished I looked up and saw my mother sitting on the couch sorting mail. I didn't know she had been there.

"That was beautiful, Abi. I really enjoy your playing." I shrugged. "We need to figure out how to get the piano over to Mom's," she continued.

"I have to have the piano," I said, my voice coming out scared when I wanted to sound firm.

"I know, Abi." She smiled reassuringly. "I know you need your piano." I felt so relieved that I actually smiled back at her.

Connecting to the Earth Can Help

Think about the center of the Earth, that red, molten, fiery still point in the center of the spinning world. Imagine a connection between your feet or the base of your spine and the center of the Earth. It could be like a very long tree root, a column of light, a gold or silver cord or chain, or whatever appeals to you. Make sure it is securely connected at both ends in the present moment. If one end or the other looks like it is floating free, just imagine attaching it by tying or plugging it in again.

Chapter 30

Jessica's Poem

Tara and I were sitting in her kitchen drinking hot chocolate when her mom came home from work. She looked tired. "Do you want some hot chocolate, Mom?" Tara asked.

"Sure." She smiled at Tara. "Let me get out of these scrubs." Tara dumped Bear out of her lap and put a mug of water in the microwave. When Tara's mom came back she was wearing jeans and a tee shirt that said, "Sail Prudhoe Bay" with a picture of a little sailboat on it. That's where Tara's dad works, but I think the tee shirt must be a joke, because from what I've heard it is so cold up there that the ocean is frozen solid most of the year.

"So how are you doing, Abi?" She asked me after she sat down with her mug. It made me feel warm inside that she wanted to know.

"Okay. My mom and I are moving to my grandma's this weekend. It will be farther for me to walk over here."

"That's too bad. I hope you'll still be able to come. I could give you a ride home sometimes."

I smiled. "Thanks, Mrs. Barker."

"You'd better just call me Anna. I feel old when you call me Mrs." She looked out the window. "I can't believe it is almost the end of May already and the leaves are just starting to come out on the birches."

"I guess I won't be going back to California this summer," I said. "I'll be stuck in Bluff with my monster mom." Tara carefully swirled the last of her hot chocolate around the bottom of her mug.

"Bluff isn't so bad in the summer. But I guess you miss your friends in California." Tara was still busy with her mug.

Betrayal

by Jessica Cornfield

Never again
will I trust anything
The way I trusted you.

Now,
in every situation
I question myself
endlessly.

The answers flee from me,
like a flock of startled birds.

They call to me.
I have no way to follow.

"It's actually my dad I miss," I said. "I don't really have any friends like you in California."

"What do you mean, like me?" Tara asked softly, still looking down.

"Oh, I don't know...the way you really know me and like me anyway." Finally Tara looked up at me and smiled.

"Are things pretty hard between you and your mom?" Anna asked, gently. I nodded.

"I think she really is trying, Abi," Anna said. I didn't say anything.

"Did you see Jessica's poem in the paper?" Tara asked. I was glad she was changing the subject. "She got first place for poetry in the Junior/Senior High category!" She handed me the Bluff News, folded open to Jessica's poem. I read it. I read it again. Then my eyes got too watery to read.

"I can't believe she wrote that," I whispered. "That's exactly the way it is."

Chapter 31

. . . .

Changes

The move was a royal pain. But Mom got some of her friends from church and her job to help, so it went pretty fast. Four of the men even moved my piano. I was a wreck, worrying about it getting dropped. A lot of our stuff was still in boxes, but I had my room pretty much the way I wanted it. It was small but at least I had my own room. My mom was sleeping on a couch in the living room.

After dinner she asked me if I wanted to play Kings in the Corners with her and Grandma. It's a card game Grandma taught me to play when I was little. It was kind of fun playing again, like we used to when Grandma visited. My mom kept passing when she could have played.

Where Are Your Personal Space Boundaries?

One exercise you could try is to have a friend stand across the room from you. Ask your friend to slowly walk toward you. As she walks toward you, notice how your body reacts (maybe butterflies in your stomach, tense jaw muscles, a headache, foot jiggling, or an uneasy or uncomfortable feeling in your chest). It's good to pay attention to these feelings so that you can recognize them when you are in a real life situation. As soon as you start to feel uncomfortable or uneasy, ask your partner to stop. Look at how close your partner is to you. The distance away from you is the distance that you need to feel safe with this trusted friend. Your space boundaries may be different with different people, or different on different days. Remember, the best space distance is the one that allows even the most scared or vulnerable part of you to feel safe.[1]

"Look on the table, Mabel," my grandma teased her like she always used to tease me. Mom shook her head and smiled at us.

"I guess my mind isn't in the game," she said. "Why don't you two keep playing while I try to get some more of this stuff organized?" She seemed friendlier to me than usual. I heard Anna's voice in my head: "She's really trying."

Then my dad called. Mom barely said hello before she handed me the phone. I put my cards down and took the phone to my room. When I heard my dad's voice I felt like I was going to start crying again, but I took a belly breath and let it out slowly.

"How would you like to come stay with your grandparents and me in California this summer?" he asked, with a smile in his voice. Relief flooded through me.

"You really want me to?" I asked.

"Of course I do, Honey."

"Do you think Mom will let me come?"

There was a pause. I hoped I hadn't said something wrong. "Your mother and I have talked it over. She wants you and I to see a shrink together. What do you think about that?" I didn't know what to say. It made me nervous to think about going to a whole new therapist. And my dad would probably just get mad and embarrass me. But what if Mom wouldn't let me go to California unless we agreed to go? Maybe the therapist would help me talk to him if he was making me feel weird.

"Do you want to see a shrink with me?" he asked again.

"I don't care," I said, hoping that they would decide, not me.

"Uh, listen, Abi." Dad sounded embarrassed. "I've been seeing someone here."

"You have a girlfriend!" I gasped.

"No, no, no." He laughed. "A shrink, a therapist. I'm giving it a try. The fellow I'm seeing says that what you and I are going through isn't that unusual. Uh, what am I trying to say here?" If he felt confused, I sure did. I didn't say anything. "Abi, I guess a lot of fathers get awkward when their little girls start changing into young women. I didn't mean to make you uncomfortable. What happened was my fault. I was meeting my own needs to be close to someone, through you. But I never meant it to feel awkward or sexual to you. Abi, you didn't do anything wrong."

"It's okay, Dad," I said. Part of me was going, NOT!, but I didn't want him to get mad at me again.

"I'll get you here somehow, Kiddo." I hoped he was right. After we hung up I got all excited about seeing my old friends and my grandparents and going to my favorite restaurants. Then I started thinking about Tara and Mike and Jake and my other friends. I had already started planning to do things with them this summer. I wished my parents had never split up. If I stayed in Bluff maybe my dad would come up to see me, and my parents would get back together. (Maybe they would just fight again.) If he came back, where would we live? The new renters were already moving into

Give Yourself a Butterfly Hug

Cross your arms, with each hand resting on the outside of the opposite arm. Now, with alternating taps, tap your right and then your left arm. This is called the "butterfly hug", and will help you to feel more calm and centered.[2]

our house. Everything seemed so complicated. My mind kept going round and around about all the problems. Finally when I was trying to fall asleep, I thought of going to my safe place in my mind. I was surprised to see a white cat curled up on the green pillows. It hadn't been there the last time. I imagined myself curled up on the pillows next to the cat, and fell asleep in real life.

At school the next few days Jake kept trying to talk to me, but I was too embarrassed. I just tried to avoid him. I wanted to be friends with him but it was too hard. I wondered if I should break up with Jake and try to get together with Mike instead. Then I could start over and not have to feel so weird. I just wanted to be normal.

Chapter 32

The Second to the Last Group

On Thursday, Carol said it was going to be the second to the last group. I couldn't believe it. At the beginning, when she said the group would last for 12 weeks, it had seemed like forever.

"But I'm not over the sexual abuse yet," I protested.

"Me either." Danielle hopped off the couch. "We should get an extension."

Carol smiled at us. "What do you mean when you say 'getting over the sexual abuse'?"

"Well, when am I going to stop wondering if there is something wrong with me when I think about guys, for one thing. And I'm only just finally starting to get angry at Phil for what he did to me," I said. "My therapist says that is good, but when will I be done with that?"

Danielle plopped back down, on the couch, curls vibrating. "Yeah, and when will I get over being

Myth: Healing from sexual abuse means that you will feel like you did before it happened.
Fact: The sexual abuse is part of your life story. Being a survivor of sexual abuse is a part of who you are. Healing has to do with being able to see and accept the big picture of your life, the easy parts as well as the difficult parts.

What if You Never Feel Angry?

Anger is very important. It activates a part of yourself that works to protect other parts that are hurt and vulnerable.

If you haven't felt any anger at all about the abuse, you may be emotionally protecting the person who abused you or the people who didn't stop the abuse and didn't protect you. Or, you may be protecting yourself from this strong feeling. You may not want to feel angry, but it is a normal and good part of the healing process.

scared to be alone? That EMDR is helping some, and I can usually go to sleep now, but I'm still way different than I was before it happened. How long do you think it will take?"

"I'm never in a million years going to be like I was before it happened," Imaya said quietly. Her jaw muscles rippled.

"I used to think that when I healed from the abuse I experienced as a child, I would go back to being like I was before the abuse." Carol said. "But once it happens, the sexual abuse is always part of a person's life story. Healing means you grow in ways you wouldn't have had to grow if you hadn't been abused. For example, think about all the practice you are getting in learning healthy ways to cope with enormously hard feelings."

"I don't care what you say, I'm never going to be glad it happened to me," I said.

"Of course not, Abi," Carol said. "I don't mean you should be glad it happened. I'm sorry if any of you thought I meant that." Imaya let out her breath in a whoosh. "I just mean that what has happened can't be undone. You will

...or You Feel Angry All the Time?

Sometimes anger that lasts for years and years can start to get in the way of having positive and healthy relationships with ourselves and others. If you feel like your anger is getting in the way of feeling whole or connecting with other people, it's time to get help working through your anger.

grow up to be a different person than you would have been if you hadn't been abused. It's a reality now."

"If they ever catch the guy who attacked me," Danielle said, "I might have to go to court."

"Eddie pled out," Imaya said. "I never had to go to court, but he hardly got any time in jail."

"Pled out? What does that mean?" I asked.

"Well, he was charged with all this stuff, assault, and four counts of sexual abuse of a minor." She pulled her sweatshirt sleeves down over her hands and wrapped her arms around her stomach. "He did more than that, but I have a hard time remembering. Everything gets all fuzzy in my mind." Danielle scooted over on the couch and put her arm around Imaya. Imaya took a breath and let it out slowly, through pursed lips. "So anyway, he said he hadn't done any of it, that I was just crazy... psycho. He said he wasn't guilty. I was really upset, and my mom was, too. Then I guess they talked him into saying he was guilty of beating me, by dropping some of the charges against him. They didn't want me to have to go through a trial. They dropped the sexual abuse charges so he only had the assault against him."

Forgetting Painful Memories

When really painful things happen to us, sometimes our minds turn off and we block the memory out (this is called dissociation). There is research that shows that many adults who were sexually abused as children don't remember the abuse after they grow up. Even when there was actual physical evidence of abuse, or when the person who offended sexually admitted to the abuse, many survivors do not remember the abuse as adults.[1]

"What?" I almost yelled, "How could they do that?"

"They didn't think he had sexually abused you?" Danielle asked.

"No, that's not it at all," Carol said. "It's called plea bargaining. They get the defendant to plead guilty by taking away some of the charges. The victim's lawyer and the abuser's lawyer both want to avoid a trial if they can. It may be that because Imaya was having a hard time remembering what happened, her lawyer was afraid they wouldn't be able to prove beyond a shadow of a doubt that Eddie was guilty of the sexual abuse. People were probably concerned about how hard a trial would be on you, Imaya." Imaya nodded.

"They had pictures of the bruises and an X-ray of my broken arm, but the sexual stuff didn't show on my body. They kept saying 'no physical evidence' about the sexual abuse," Imaya went on.

I was feeling sick to my stomach about what Imaya was saying. Bruises and a broken arm and sexual abuse so bad she couldn't even bear to remember it. Eddie should have been locked up forever or tortured to death. Danielle spoke my thoughts.

Myth: Everybody needs the same things to help them heal.
Fact: Abuse hurts people in different ways. Everyone heals in their own ways. You might need to tell about what happened to you over and over, or only once. You might think about it all the time, or you might not be able to remember what happened. You might need to make loud noises and hit pillows and cry and dream and sing and write poems and paint and talk, or just some of those things. You might need a lot of help from other people, or you might work through it mostly on your own.

"It's not fair. They should at the very least have locked Eddie up for life for what he did."

"I wish," Imaya said quietly.

"You've had so many bad things happen to you already, I wish you wouldn't be so mean to yourself with making your arms bleed and stuff. You deserve to have only the nicest things happen to you for the rest of your life," I said.

"Whatever," Imaya said, like she was a little angry with me.

"We are all doing the best we can," Carol said quietly. Imaya looked at Carol.

"My therapist says that when I cut my arms it is a part of me trying to take care of myself, but doing it in a way that makes it confusing for other people to understand how it could be self protection. She says that it does help to protect me from feeling all the feelings about the abuse, but that, since it also hurts me, she wants me to find new ways to protect myself."

She was still looking at Carol, so hopefully she didn't see my confusion. She kept going. "There are parts of me that are still so injured and scared from when Eddie was hurting me that they don't understand that I'm safe now. I have some parts of myself that want to hurt me because they feel I deserve it. Other parts are doing the hurting because they are trying to distract me from the bigger horror of the memories of being abused."

"I have parts like that," Jessica said. "When I eat too much, I'm trying to drown out those sad and angry voices inside."

Imaya smiled at her. "When I talked to the transitional housing lady about letting mom and me stay longer, I had to have the scared and screaming parts step back so my truest and best self could speak up." She paused. "That's the part of me that knows how to be a friend to myself!"

"We all have parts of ourselves that want to run away or that react to scary situations, sometimes by hurting ourselves or others," Carol said. "We also have parts that take care of us, sort of manage our day-to-day interactions and get us doing the things that we are expected to do. And we all have parts that are deeply hidden. Those parts often hold the most difficult memories or feelings from past events."

Carol turned to look at Imaya, then glanced at each of us before going on. "Even when it seems like one particular part of ourselves, a destructive or unfeeling part, for example, is usually in control, we can learn to function from a more whole or peaceful place. When we lead all our different parts from a true sense of self we are calm, centered, and we can care about ourselves and others. Some of you might want to talk more with your therapists about how your different parts interact with each other and how you can learn to be in your core self more often."

It was quiet. I was trying to figure out if I had any reactive or destructive parts like Imaya and Jessica were talking about. I wasn't sure at all what my "true self" was, or if I even had one. I decided to think about it later, when I was by myself.

"Do you want us to come, if you have to go to trial?" I asked Danielle.

"Would you really come? If I saw you there I would remember to breathe."
We made sure we all had each other's phone numbers again.

I couldn't let go. I wanted us to keep meeting. "But we still need the group."
I said to Carol, almost begging. "I need a safe place to talk to everyone. I have so many questions. I don't know how to talk to my dad. I don't know how to be with boys. It's like Jessica said, the answers are all flying away from me!"

Jessica looked startled. I took a breath. "I loved your poem, Jessica." Her blue eyes looked back at mine for a moment before she looked down, maybe wondering if she could believe me, maybe wondering why in the world I would ever say anything nice to her. I watched her, thinking that she was someone I would like to get to know, wondering if I'd blown all my chances.

"I cut it out and put it in my jewelry box," Tara said. Everyone chimed in about how good the poem was. Jessica laughed and covered her mouth, turning pinker by the minute.

"Could we please change the subject?" she asked, her voice shaking a little.

Carol smiled at her. "You are brave and talented, Jessica. I hope you will keep writing and publishing your work." Then she looked at me. "Just because this group is ending, it doesn't mean you should now have all the answers, or that you won't need support."

"And I never thanked Jessica for telling the school counselor about Phil," I said, looking at Carol. "She probably thinks I still blame her." Carol raised her eyebrows at me with a small smile and held her hands palms up toward me and then toward Jessica as if she were offering to pass a gift between us. Jessica was looking down, clutching her notebook with both hands.

"I'm sorry, Jessica, I really am. It was Phil that hurt me and confused me, not you. He was the pervert. You were the heroine. I don't know why I blamed you. I was stupid. I'm sorry."

Wet splotches were appearing on Jessica's notebook. Finally Jessica started shaking her head slowly, tears still falling.

"This is too much for me," she whispered. "I need to write about it. I don't know what to think."

Chapter 33

Trees

The day after school was out, I bicycled over to Tara's. We were planning to bike out to the place where the forest fire had been. Anna and Tara were in the kitchen putting together some snacks for us to bring. I guess seeing me reminded Tara about what we'd talked about at group.

"I've been wondering, Mom, why didn't James have to be in a trial?" Tara asked.

"Because he admitted to what he'd done."

"He said he was guilty?" Tara obviously didn't believe her.

"Well, yes, Tara, he admitted he was pressuring you and threatening you. Didn't you know that?"

"He always told me he would say that I wanted it. That's why I was afraid to tell anyone." She sat down at the table. Bear put his paws on her knees and tried to lick her face. Tara put her chin up to avoid his tongue and wrapped her fingers behind his ears. "Some of my cousins say I probably wanted it. I thought that's what he's been telling everyone."

"I don't know, Honey." Her mother said, suddenly looking very old. "I don't know what he's been telling them, but I'll talk with him about it tonight. He told us he knew it was his fault."

"Then why didn't he have to go to jail? I know you must have told his therapist what he did. I thought sexual abuse was supposed to be against the law."

Anna sighed. "He is too young to go to adult jail. The probation officer didn't recommend residential treatment or the youth prison. The judge went with the probation officer's recommendation. But he is still on probation, and he was ordered to see a therapist here in Bluff. And we aren't allowed to let him be around any younger children without an adult around."

How Will I Know When I've Healed?

You will be able to think and talk about the abuse.
You will be able to think and talk about things other than the abuse.
You will sleep pretty normally.
You'll be able to concentrate in school.
You'll feel comfortable being assertive, or standing up for yourself.
You'll feel comfortable leaving your house.
You will experience joy.
You will be able to tolerate someone touching your shoulder or shaking your hand.
You will be able to bathe normally, without experiencing shame or thinking that you are "dirty."
You will be interested in your future.
You will start conversations with others.

Continued on page 192

How Will I Know When I've Healed? *continued*

You will be able to handle someone criticizing you without feeling shame.

You will be able to tell the difference between supportive and non-supportive relationships.

You will choose supportive relationships.

You will be able to tolerate strong emotions in others and in yourself.

You will have a positive body image.

You will be able to relax without using drugs or alcohol.

You will look for fun things to do by yourself and with others.

You will care about and show concern for other people.

You will be able to remember recent and past events.

You will be able to express your anger in a healthy way.

You will feel confident that you have value.

You will laugh.

You will trust yourself.

You will have a healthy appetite and you will eat when you are hungry.

You will take care of yourself physically and emotionally.

You will have a sense of your own personal space.

You will feel good about yourself.

You will be able to feel sad about things that are sad, and it will have nothing to do with the abuse.

Don't worry if you don't feel all of these things all the time; none of us do. The idea is that you start to feel some of these things some of the time, and then most of these things most of the time. Healing is a process, but it can and does happen! [1]

"I knew he was talking to a therapist about what he did, but I didn't know he was on probation," Tara said. She seemed kind of pleased about it.

"Some day, if his therapist thinks he's ready and your therapist thinks you are ready, you and he may talk together about what happened," Tara's mom said, getting a package of cookies out of the cupboard. Tara looked shocked.

What Happens When You Don't Tell?

Bad things have to be worked through in some way. If you feel like you can't share the abuse with anyone, you can't truly work through it, and it doesn't get any better. When you try to hold the feelings about the abuse inside your body, they just leak out — usually in anger problems, substance abuse, depression, nightmares, flashbacks, or illness.

As hard as it may be to ask for help, you deserve it! Keep asking for help until you find someone who believes you, values you, and helps you to heal.

"I'm not ready for that," she whispered. Her mom nodded.

"That's okay, Honey. It's okay if you never are." She opened the package and offered it to Tara and me then took three for herself and set the bag on the table.

"I shouldn't be eating these," she said with a faint smile.

"I don't really like the therapist I have now, Mom," Tara said. "I liked Lucy. She was easy to talk to. I wish she hadn't moved away. I don't think the one I have now really likes me."

Anna looked surprised. "Hmm. Maybe you could give her another week or two. Sometimes it takes a while to get used to a new therapist. Meanwhile, I'll check into other possibilities. Okay?" Tara nodded.

Her mother sighed. "I'm glad we're finally talking about this now, Tara, even though it's hard for me. When I was growing up I didn't talk to anyone about the abuse. I felt just so alone. Sometimes I don't know how I survived." Her eyes were far away. "Now our Elders are saying that talking about it will help us heal.

Our tribal leaders are saying that to stop child sexual abuse in our community, we must break the silence. We're starting to talk about all the old secrets, about historical trauma and boarding schools, and where some of the sexual abuse came from." She sighed and shook her head, then looked at us. "My own daughter is teaching me the wisdom of the Elders."

I started to laugh, but I noticed that Tara had tears in her eyes. Tara's mom noticed too. "We'll just keep on talking about it as much as we need to, girls."

Tara jumped up. "But I don't want everyone talking about me!"

Anna looked startled. "Breaking the silence doesn't mean everyone gossiping about what happened to you, Tara. Breaking the silence means that adults stop pretending like sexual abuse doesn't happen here in Bluff. It means that adults figure out ways to help victims and families heal. It means that victims like both of you girls, and also James and Theresa and me, find Elders and others willing to listen and help us heal if we choose to talk. It means education, so that children know that sexual abuse is against the law and how to get help if it is happening to them. It means parents talking to their children about abuse, and parents knowing where their children are and who is with them." I think she would have gone

> ## Trusting Your Therapist
> Trust takes time, and both you and your therapist should allow for the time that is necessary to build trust. If you don't feel comfortable right at first, that's pretty normal, but if you don't feel comfortable after several meetings (or sessions), you might want to look for another therapist. Here are some important things to look for in a therapist:
> - Someone who is knowledgeable and skilled in sexual abuse treatment.
> - Someone you can learn to trust.
> - Someone who doesn't judge, threaten, intimidate, lecture, or scare you.
> - Someone who is comfortable talking about sex and sexuality.

on and on, but she noticed we were inching toward the door and the sunshine. After we hugged her, she tried to hold and comfort Bear while we squeezed out the door. It felt great to be on our bikes with the freedom of summer ahead of us.

I thought the forest fire area would be black everywhere, with charred trees and ashes on the ground. There were a lot of blackened tree skeletons, their branches making patterns against the sky, but some of the trees were still alive, scorched on one side but with new buds starting to open. Just above the black ground a cloud of green floated, made from all the new little plants coming up through the ashes.

Elder

In many Alaska Native cultures, a respected individual who has aged past 50 years, and lived a life that has been respectful of the land, culture, and other individuals, is considered an "Elder." An Elder holds certain knowledge, beliefs, and values which he or she passes on to the younger generations. A true Elder does not abuse other people. Someone who is considered an Elder but who abuses others is acting out of hypocrisy. People who appear to be one thing, but are not, (similar to a therapist, a youth pastor, or a teacher who is supposed to be a role model but betrays the mission or role they hold) are abusing their power and your trust. When community members find out, these people are generally considered "Olders,", or older people, rather than "Elders."

We laid our bikes against some trees on the other side of the road, and then walked into the burned area. Being around all the dead trees made my heart hurt. I looked at Tara. She looked solemn.

"There is a lot of power here," she said quietly.

"What do you mean?" I asked.

"I don't know exactly. It's weird, like I can almost see the flames." She shook her head and her hair flew out. "How can all these plants have come up so quickly?"

"I'd be scared to come up again, if I was a plant. I'd just want to stay down underground so I wouldn't get burned again," I said.

"That's another thing about the power. It's like they are more eager than ever to reach and grow and gather sunlight and everything. It must have something to do with the roots and seeds underground. All the stuff happening that we never even see."

"I don't see how they can just come up again after what happened. The smoke and flames! It must have been terrifying to not be able to run. I'd hate to be a plant." I reached down and patted one of the plants gently so it wouldn't take it personally.

"Sometimes I feel like that," Tara said. "Sometimes I just want to hide somewhere safe. But sometimes, I want to be like the plants, I want to keep coming back up. I want to be here in the world, even though awful things happen. I want to reach up toward the sun. I want to have deep roots that connect me to the earth and help me to survive."

"You don't have roots," I said, looking at her tennis shoes, gray from the ashes.

Being a Tree

Imagining being a tree can help you feel your own power and strength. It will help you open to the support that is available around you like sunshine. You can do this anywhere: sitting or standing, inside or outdoors. Remember to keep breathing.

Imagine you are a tree. Take a deep belly breath and let it out slowly. Feel the warm sun on your branches, and a breeze gently ruffling your leaves. Breathe. Listen to the sounds of the birds. Take a deep breath and then let it out slowly. Notice your trunk at your center. It is a highway for energy moving up and down between heaven and earth. Breathe. Reach your tree roots deep, deep into the earth. Breathe.

Sense the water and other nutrients that are available deep underground. Take a belly breath and let it out slowly. Allow the minerals and water from deep in the earth to flow up through your roots, up your trunk, and into your branches and leaves. Breathe. Feel your leaves fluttering in the sunshine. Take a deep breath and let it out slowly. Enjoy the feeling of being a tree.

Tara and I wrote this one together. Abi

"I know. But in a way I feel like I do. It's hard to describe. You think I'm crazy, don't you, Abi?" She looked at me without smiling.

"No." A picture formed in my mind. "If we were trees, I'll bet our roots would be touching underground."

Tara smiled. "Yes."

More Stuff

You Might Want To Know

For a Resource List of books and websites please go to **www.neari.com/press** and look under the book's title "The Thursday Group".

What Is Sexual Abuse?

- Asking a child to do anything sexual, including looking at movies, websites, books, magazines or pictures of sex (pornography).

- Taking the child's picture in a way that sexually excites an adult.

- Touching a child in their private areas (genitals, breasts, bottom), even with clothes on.

- Having the child touch the adult or older child's private parts, even with clothes on.

- Putting anything into the child's vagina (front opening) or anus (back opening).

- Having the child put anything into the adult or older child's vagina or anus.

- Having a child watch or listen to other people have sex.

Understanding Privacy (Confidentiality) in Therapy

If you are under 18, the therapist you're working with may be required to share some of what you say with your parent or guardian. This usually includes only general information about what you are discussing, such as "issues about anger" or "family patterns," but different therapists share different amounts of information with parents. It is important to ask your therapist how much he or she will share with your parents so that you know how open you want to be.

If you are in the custody of the state, the therapist may have to share these same things with your social worker or juvenile probation officer. In these situations, the therapist may or may not be required to share the same information with your parents. Be sure to ask for more details if you have any questions.

If the sexual abuse case goes to court, the therapist may be required to testify and sometimes is unable to keep everything you have said private. There may be ways your therapist can keep from having to testify, but if he or she ultimately does testify, your therapist should work with you ahead of time so that you have an idea of what will be said in court, and won't be surprised.

If you tell your therapist that you or any child has been hurt or neglected, or about sexual abuse that hasn't been reported, the therapist will be required by law to report the abuse to child protection services or to the police.

If you say that you are going to kill yourself or someone else, the therapist cannot keep this private; she or he will have to break your confidentiality in order to keep you and/or others safe.

If you are worried about what kind of information your therapist can keep confidential, be sure to ask for a clear explanation so that you feel safe sharing your personal information.

Some Legal Stuff You Should Know

There may be a Victim Advocate, Victim Coordinator, or Guardian ad Litem helping the prosecutor to get you and your family ready for court. This is a good person to ask questions about anything related to court that you don't understand or want more information about. If a parent is not able to help you deal with court, you can ask another adult to go with you to court or anything related to the legal system.

In Alaska, or other rural settings, you may participate in a Grand Jury hearing by phone because it is not available in your home town. In a Grand Jury hearing, there will be lawyers for the state (the District Attorney) and lawyers for the defendant (the Defense Attorney), as well as a jury of 12 or more people and a judge. You will be asked to talk to the group and tell them what you know about what happened. The lawyers will be able to ask you questions, but the defendant (often referred to as the "alleged" abuser) will not be there. This forum is meant to determine whether there is enough evidence to go forward with a full criminal trial.

If you have to go to trial, the people in the courtroom will include the prosecuting attorney, the defense attorney, the defendant, the judge and the jury. The defendant's family and friends may be there as well. You can have a family member or advocate with you when you go in to talk about what happened (testify) unless he/she is also a witness.

You should be able to go into the courtroom and look around before you have to go in to testify. If you can't go into the room, you may be able to look at a model (like a child's doll house), or a photograph of a courtroom. Or, you can have someone help you draw a picture of the courtroom, including where each person will be seated, and where the jury will be. Knowing what the court room looks like and where you and other people will be seated will help you to feel more confident and assured when you have to testify.

One hard thing to understand is that the law can say that something is wrong, but the lawyers and jury may not look at the evidence (facts) in the same way. Just because the abuser doesn't go to jail does not mean that the lawyers or jury didn't believe you and it doesn't mean that the abuser didn't break the law. It never means the abuse didn't happen.

I didn't know about having all these rights. Abi

When You Have to Go to Court

You can ask someone to take you to visit the courthouse or courtroom before the hearing or trial so that you can get a feel for what things look like and where you or other people will be in the courtroom.

You can wear whatever you want to court. You don't have to be dressed up. Wear something you will feel comfortable wearing. You can also bring your favorite stuffed animal, wear "power jewelry" (like a bracelet or necklace that helps you to feel powerful or confident), or bring something to hold in your hands while you testify.

It is a good idea to get a good night's sleep* and to eat something light before you go to court.

Exercise is a great way to help you feel better about yourself in general, but it can also help to decrease your emotional and physical response to talking about the abuse. It's a good idea to start an exercise program as soon as you hear that you might have to go to court (or even if you never go to court). Even if it's only a few minutes a day, regular exercise will help you to deal with the emotions that are likely to come up when you testify.

Both the District Attorney and the Defense Attorney (the lawyers) will ask you questions while you are sitting on "the stand" (the witness box located near the judge's seat). Some of the questions they ask you will be hard to answer. It will probably be uncomfortable to talk about the abuse. Even though it may be hard, the information you give will be important information for the court.

*Hah. Abi

If you don't know the answer to a question it is okay to say that you don't know. Don't try to guess at the right answer or make something up.

You have the right to ask for more information if you don't understand what you are being asked or if you don't understand a word that was used.

You can take as much time as you need when answering questions. Remember to breathe.

Ask your parent, advocate, or therapist to help you think of ways to sit and to hold your hands that will make you feel as comfortable as possible.

If you need more time to think or calm down, take 5 or 10 deep belly breaths, or think of your safe place or something that makes you feel calm or happy.

If you need to go to the bathroom, or need a drink of water, it's okay to ask for a time out. You can tell the judge you need a break, or have a signal you use with your advocate.

If you forget something, it's okay. You can say you forgot.

If you need to cry, go ahead and cry.

Talking to someone about the things you are worried about regarding court and how you feel ahead of time can help you to feel better. Good people to talk to can include a supportive family member, your therapist, guardian ad litem or victim advocate.

The person who abused you is not allowed to talk to you before, during, or after court. He is never allowed to get near you or to touch you at any time. Guards are in the courtroom to enforce this.

During testimony, you do not have to look at the person who abused you, but can focus instead on the judge, the lawyer who is speaking to you, the guards in the room, or anyone else that you choose. If you get scared, look at someone you trust, like your advocate or a supportive parent.

You are not testifying for or against the person who abused you. Your testimony is simply giving the judge and jury information that will be helpful to them in making good decisions about the future.

After you testify, go to lunch or for a snack or a drive with someone special (like your mom, your guardian ad litem, or therapist) or do something special for yourself. Be sure to tell a caring adult all about it. [1]

A Physical Exam

When sexual abuse includes touching or having sex, it can leave tiny marks, tears, or other evidence on a person's body. If you were touched under your clothing, or experienced skin to skin contact, during sexual abuse, you may be asked to have a physical exam.

A physical exam is specifically an exam of the pelvic area. You will be asked to lie back on a table, with your legs apart so that the nurse examiner can check your private areas. Sometimes a special camera allows nurses to see the exam area up close. An exam may also be videotaped or photographed for use as evidence (in a court room) later. This information may be helpful in determining who the abuser was, when the abuse took place, and what type of abuse occurred. You should be told about it beforehand if a camera or video will be used.

Examiners will use a special light to check for signs of health and injury. You will be told about any difficulties or injuries that are found. For some, this feels very scary and it can be hard to go through. For others, it is a relief to know their body is normal and fine.

You may be wondering why a nurse or police officer would insist on an exam, or not take your word for what happened. Some children who have been abused don't remember all of what happened, or they're feeling too scared or ashamed to tell. Because of this, an exam can be a good idea even when you don't feel physically hurt or don't think it's needed.

You may want someone that you trust to be with you during the exam so that you feel more comfortable. Tell the nurse or doctor if you feel uncomfortable, need to stop, or to take a break. Even though this exam is very important in order to make sure that you do not need any immediate physical care, it is also important for you to feel that you are in control if you need it to stop.

Sometimes people think that the abuse was not very serious if there is no physical evidence, but the fact is that only 4 percent of rape victims receive serious physical injuries[2] and fewer than that show physical injuries if they have been molested. Vaginal and anal tissue heals very quickly, so that, even when there are injuries, they are often not visible after 48 hours.

It still seems like they didn't believe me about what happened. Abi

What Happens After I Tell?

If you tell a "Mandated Reporter" about the abuse, he/she is required by law to make a report to the proper authorities (that's what "mandated reporter" means). Mandated Reporters include anyone whose job is helping or working with children, and anyone who works in an agency that helps or works with children in any way. Sometimes friends, neighbors, or family members also choose to make a report when they learn about child abuse, even if they aren't mandated reporters.

Child sexual abuse is reported to Child Protective Services if the abuser is someone in your immediate family who lives with you, or if someone in your immediate family knew about the abuse and didn't protect you. If this happens, you will usually have a social worker assigned to help your family.

If the person who abused you was a stranger, a family friend, or a family member who doesn't live in your home, then the report will go to law enforcement (local police, sheriff, or state troopers).

If charges are brought against the person who abused you, then your family may be in contact with the District Attorney's office, since it is this office that decides whether a case will go to court. Even if you say that the abuse didn't happen, the District Attorney, and not you or your family, is the person who will decide whether someone who is accused of sexual abuse will be charged with a crime and have to go to court.

Sometimes reports need to be made to both child protection services and the police. If the person who abused you was between the ages of 13 and17, there will probably be a juvenile probation officer and other juvenile court personnel involved as well. These systems are all complicated and have their own rules and time lines.

Because these systems are so complicated, it's a good idea to ask your therapist, social worker, victim's advocate, guardian ad litem, or prosecuting attorney to help you understand more about what is going to happen in your particular situation. You have a right to know!

Tara asked me to put this in the book. She got it for me from her therapist. Abi

Sex Offender Treatment Programs

Sex offender treatment programs look at the way a person who has been convicted of a sex offense thinks and acts. They also address the way that person believes, what his values are, and what kinds of habits he has formed. This type of therapy is designed to change the thinking errors that help the offender excuse, deny, or justify his behavior. The therapy will also set up safety plans with the person who abuses and his support system to reduce the chances that he or she will behave in a sexually abusive manner again.

Until recently it was believed that people who offended sexually would never change. There are studies now that show that some types of offenses can be greatly reduced with specialized therapy.[3] In general, people who are most likely to benefit from that kind of therapy include adolescents and adults who have not yet set up a long-time pattern of abusing others. When there is lots of violence with the abuse, or when there is a pattern of abuse (many victims or the same type of abuse repeated over time), the person who offends may not benefit as much from therapy.[4]

Sex offender treatment (therapy) can happen in prison, in long-term residential treatment programs and in outpatient therapy settings. The type of treatment a person receives varies depending upon how he abused, what he was convicted of, and what is known about his offense pattern. Sometimes the treatment depends upon what is available in a given area.

Prison treatment can be provided only if the person who offended has been sentenced to a certain period of time in jail or in a juvenile detention center. There has to be a treatment program available in the prison that the offender is sentenced to, and the offender usually has to agree to attend treatment and admit to his crime. Sometimes treatment is required by the court.

Residential treatment is typically available only to people under the age of 18 who have committed a sexual offense, and have been adjudicated (tried and convicted) of a sex crime. Residential treatment is available in just a few states, and in even fewer cities and towns. Because of this shortage, adolescents who need this treatment often have to leave their state to get it. Treatment often lasts a year or longer, and includes at least one hour of individual therapy and several hours of group therapy every week. Family therapy is also usually required, and sometimes other types of therapies are included as well.

Outpatient sex offender therapy can be individual, group, or family therapy, or some combination of all three. In intensive outpatient therapy, all three are required and the person who offended must attend a certain number of hours of therapy per week. Usually a person doing this type of therapy also has a probation or parole officer. Both adolescents and adults can go through this type of therapy.

Understanding Sexuality and Relationships/Dating After Sexual Abuse

When a person has been sexually abused, it can mess with the way that they think and feel.

Bodies can have a way of acting all on their own, even when our brains don't want them to. People who have been sexually abused often feel that their bodies have "betrayed" them because they responded to the touching.

After the abuse, touching that is supposed to feel good can feel yucky, disgusting, or overwhelming. This can make it hard to be sexual even with someone you love and trust. Another thing bodies do is to feel "turned on," or hypersexual, at times that you might wish they wouldn't. Sometimes it can feel like you are aroused all the time, or at really inappropriate times.

Talking to a therapist, practicing yoga, karate, or other types of exercise, and getting some body work (such as a therapeutic massage, for example) can help to change these automatic body responses to sexual touches and thoughts.

Our minds can do similar things, and make us feel just as out of control. After sexual abuse, it can be hard to trust others. This makes it difficult to be close with friends or in intimate or loving relationships. Sometimes people even do things to get the loved one to leave them, hurt them, or think of them as ugly and stupid, because that is how they think of themselves.

Other times, the sexual abuse can make a person want to be close to others in a sexual way, because this is the only way that they know how to get someone's attention, or because they confuse love and sex. Or, sometimes, it is because they believe that sex is the only thing that they are good for, or good at.

Sexual abuse can prompt some people to trust others in this really odd way, where they will talk to anyone and tell anyone about the abuse, get close to people really fast, and trust people who are clearly not safe. It can be really confusing to others when a person acts this way, and usually it's just as confusing to the person herself!

All of these things are normal reactions to having been sexually abused. But feeling messed up like this can really make a person upset and confused. If you are struggling with any of these things, talking to a therapist can be helpful.

Is It Harder for Boys to Tell?

Boys and men in America are often taught that they should be tough, independent, and self-sufficient. They are not taught how to seek help when they feel inadequate, vulnerable, or taken advantage of. When they are abused, they (like many girls) often think that they should have done something to stop the abuse. Telling someone about the abuse is much harder if you think that you should have done something to stop it.

It is believed that boys are most frequently abused by men, although reports of female abusers are increasing.[5] If abused by a male, boys sometimes worry that they will be seen as homosexual or that they might be homosexual. If they were abused by a woman, they might think that they should have liked the abuse, or they might be worried that other people will think they did like it or should have liked it. Boys are more likely than girls to see themselves as responsible for the abuse, and boys are less likely to be seen by others as a "victim" of sexual abuse.

Girls are more frequently abused than boys, and are more likely than boys to report sexual abuse.[6] We don't really know for sure why this is true, but we do know that, overall, boys have a harder time dealing with sexual abuse. This may be in part because boys are more likely to become physiologically aroused during an abuse situation, even when they are repulsed by what is happening.[7] Boys can have an erection and can ejaculate even when they do not want the sexual attention that they are receiving.

Boys who have been sexually abused are more likely than girls who have been sexually abused to try to kill themselves. They are also more likely to abuse alcohol and drugs.[8]

The more I find out about sexual abuse, the sadder, and madder I get. But when I talk to people about it, like Tara and her mom or our group, I feel less scared and alone. Abi

Sexual Abuse by Females

Our society has a hard time believing that a woman could sexually abuse a child because we tend to think of women as nurturing caregivers. Women as sexual abusers is a concept that has been dismissed, disbelieved, or ignored until relatively recently. This may make it even harder for people who have been abused by a woman to talk about or report the abuse.

According to current research, most of the people we know about who commit sexual abuse are males. But women and adolescent girls do abuse.[9] They abuse boys and they abuse girls. They abuse strangers, children who just happen to be in the wrong place at the wrong time, children they are related to or with whom they are friends of the parents, and they abuse their own children, just like men who abuse. One of the hardest things for people to believe, even people who treat male sex offenders, is that a woman can abuse her own children. But they can, and some do. Sexual violations by mothers may be easily denied or overlooked because of their usual caretaking roles (dressing children, diapering, being in the bathroom when a child is bathing, etc.) When mothers do abuse their children, it can be particularly difficult for the children to tell about the abuse.

Compared to what researchers know about men who abuse, there is very little data about females who abuse sexually. No one really knows what percentage of abusers are women, but one researcher estimated that 1.5 million females and 1.6 million males in this country may have been sexually abused by a woman.[10]

There aren't good specialized assessment tools or treatment options for females who abuse. Little research has been conducted with women who abuse. Training for therapists and treatment providers on what to look for in a female who may be sexually abusive is generally not available. Fortunately, we are beginning to recognize this problem, but more needs to be done.

Endnotes

Introduction:

1) Matsakis, A. (1996). *I can't get over it: A handbook for trauma survivors* (2nd ed.). Oakland, CA: New Harbinger Publications.

Chapter 1: What is Normal Anyway?
Text Box: What Kind of People Abuse?

1) Hillman, D. & Solek-Tefft, J. 1988. *Spiders and flies: help for parents and teachers of sexually abused children.* Toronto: Lexington.

Telling It Like It Is: Things you need to know about relationships, marriage, and parenting (April 3, 2008). *Child sexual abuse-facts vs. myths.* Retrieved November 24, 2008, from http://www.tellinitlikeitis.net/2008/04/child-sexual-abuse-facts-vs-myths.html

Chapter 2: Grand Jury Pages
Text Box: Shame, Secrecy, and Isolation

1) *Darkness to Light* (n.d.). Statistics surrounding child sexual abuse. Retrieved November 24, 2008, from http://www.darkness2light.org/KnowAbout/statistics_2.asp.

National Victim Center and National Crime Victims Research and Treatment Center (1992). *Rape in America: A report to the nation,* Arlington VA: Author.

Parents for Meagan's Law and the Crime Victims Center (n.d.). Statistics-child sexual abuse. Retrieved November 24, 2008, from http://www.parentsformeganslaw.org/public/statistics_childSexualAbuse.html

Chapter 4: Maybe I Could Use a Little Support
Text Box: Myth: Sexual abuse only happens to other people.

1) Bolen, R.M. (2001). *Child Sexual Abuse: Its scope and our failure* (p 270). New York: Springer-Verlag.

Demause, L. (1982). *Foundations of psychohistory.* New York: Creative Roots.

Telling It Like It Is: Things you need to know about relationships, marriage, and parenting (April 25, 2008). *Child sexual abuse: Blaming mothers of sexually abused children.* Retrieved November 24, 2008, from http://www.tellinitlikeitis.net/2008/04/child-sexual-abuse-blaming-mothers-of-sexually-abused-children.html

Chapter 5: It's Too Much!

1) *Child Welfare League of America* (January 31, 2008). Retrieved November 20, 2008 from http://ndas.cwla.org/data_stats/states/Data_Trends/Alaska%20State%20Data%20Trends.pdf

Department of Public Safety/Alaska Council on Domestic Violence and Sexual Assault Annual Report for FY 2007. Retrieved November 20, 2008 from www.dps.state.ak.us/Cdvsa/docs/AnnualReport2007.pdf

Amnesty International (2007). *Maze of Injustice: The failure to protect Indigenous women from sexual violence in the U.S.* Retrieved on November 20, 2008 from http://www.amnestyusa.org/women/maze/report.pdf.

2) Text Box: Sexual Abuse By Females

Dube, S.R., Anda, R.F., Whitfield, C.L., Brown, D.W., Felitti, V.J., Dong, M. & Giles, W.H. (2005). Long term consequences of childhood sexual abuse by gender of victim. *American Journal of Preventative Medicine,* 28(5), 430-438.

Frey, L. (2006). *Girls don't do that, do they? Adolescent females who sexually abuse.* In R.E. Longo & D.S. Prescott (Eds.), Current perspectives: Working with sexually aggressive youth and youth with sexual behavior problems (pp 119-141). Holyoke, MA: NEARI Press

Hislop, J. (2001). *Female sex offenders: What therapists, law enforcement and child protective services need to know.* Ravendale, WA,: Issues Press.

Turner, J. & Maryanski, *A. Incest: Origins of the Taboo.* Boulder, CO: Paradigm Press.

Vandiver, D.M. & Walker, J.T. (2002). Female sex offenders: An overview and analysis of 40 cases. *Criminal Justice Review,* 27, 284-300.

Whealin, J. (2003). *Child sexual abuse: A National Center for PTSD fact sheet.* Washington, D.C.: Department of Veterans Affairs.

Whealin JM (2004). *Men and sexual trauma: A National Center for PTSD fact sheet.* Birmingham, Ala.: Employee Education System, Department of Veterans Affairs.

3) Text Box: A Few Facts About Sexual Abuse

Darkness to Light (n.d.). Statistics surrounding child sexual abuse. Retrieved November 24, 2008, from http://www.darkness2light.org/KnowAbout/statistics_2.asp.

Estes, R.J. & Weiner, N.A. (2002). *The Commercial Sexual Exploitation of Children in the U.S., Canada and Mexico: Executive summary of the U.S. National Study.* Philadelphia, Pennsylvania: University of Pennsylvania, School of Social Work Center for the Study of Youth Policy.

Parents for Meagan's Law and the Crime Victims Center (n.d.). Statistics-child sexual abuse. Retrieved November 24, 2008, from http://www.parentsformeganslaw.org/public/statistics_childSexualAbuse.html

Text Box: Why Do People React Differently to the Same Type of Abuse?

4) *Banyard,* V.L. (2003). Explaining links between sexual abuse and psychological distress: Identifying mediating processes. Child Abuse & Neglect, 27, 869-875.

Cavanagh Johnson, T., & Doonan, R. (2006). *Children twelve and younger with sexual behavior problems: What we know in 2005 that we didn't know in 1985.* In R.E. Longo & D.S. Prescott (Eds.), *Current perspectives: Working with sexually aggressive youth and youth with sexual behavior problems* (pp 119-141). Holyoke, MA: NEARI Press.

Gil, E. & Cavanaugh Johnson, T. (1993). *Sexualized children: Assessment and treatment of sexualized children and children who molest.* Rockville, MD: Launch Press.

Kendall-Tackett, K. A., Williams, L. M., & Finkelhor, D. (1993). *Impact of sexual abuse on children: A review and synthesis of recent empirical studies.* Psychological Bulletin, 113(1), 164-180.

Roth, S., & Newman, E. (1993). The process of coping with incest for adult survivors: Measurement and implications for treatment and research. *Journal of Interpersonal Violence*, 8(3).

Roth, S., Newman, E., Pelcovitz, D., van der Kolk, B., & Mandel, F.S. (1997). Complex PTSD in victims exposed to sexual and physical abuse: Results from DSM-IV field trials for posttraumatic stress disorder. *Journal of Traumatic Stress*, 10, 539-555.

Roth, S., & Newman, E. (1992). The role of helplessness in recovery from sexual trauma. Canadian *Journal of Behavioral Science,* 24, 220-232.

Chapter 7: Why Does Sexual Abuse Happen?
Text Box: Myth: It happened because the person who abused was using alcohol or drugs

1) Abbey, A., Zawacki, T., Buck, P.O., Clinton, .M., McAuslan, P. (2001). Alcohol and sexual assault. *Alcohol Health and Research World*, 25(1), Retrieved November 20, 2008 from http://www.athealth.com/Practitioner/ceduc/alc_assault.html

Critchlow (1983). Blaming the booze: the attribution of responsibility for drunken behavior. *Personality and Social Psychology Bulletin*, 23, 1574-1586.

Grice, D.E., Brady, K.T., & Dustan, L.R. (1994). PTSD, victimization and substance abuse. *American Journal of Psychiatry,* Unpublished paper.

Jehu, D., Gazan, M., & Klassen, C. (1984/85). Common therapeutic targets among women who were sexually abused. *Journal of Social Work and Human Sexuality*, 3. 25-45.

Richardson, D, & Campbell, J.L. (1982). Alcohol and rape: the effect of alcohol on attributions of blame for rape. *Personality and Social Psychology Bulletin*, 8, 468-476.

Text Box: Myth: It probably won't happen again.

2) *Alaska Department of Corrections Offender Programs* (1996). Sex offender treatment program: Initial recidivism study executive summary. Anchorage: Alaska Justice Statistical Analysis Center, Justice Center, University of Alaska.

Darkness to Light (n.d.). Statistics surrounding child sexual abuse. Retrieved November 24, 2008, from http://www.darkness2light.org/KnowAbout/statistics_2.asp.

Elliot, D.S., Huizinga, D., & Morse, B.J. (1985). *The dynamics of deviant behavior: A national survey progress report.* Boulder, CO: Behavioral Research Institute.

Text Box: Myth: It probably won't happen again.

3) Center for Sex Offender Management (August 2000). *Myths and facts about sex offenders.* Retrieved November 22, 2008, from http://www.csom.org/pubs/mythsfacts.html

Langstrom, N. and M. Grann (2000). Risk for criminal recidivism among young sex offenders. *Journal of Interpersonal Violence* 15(8): 855-871.

Snyder, H.N. (2000). *Sexual assaults of young children as reported to law enforcement: Victim, incident, and offender characteristics.* Washington, D.C.: Bureau of Justice Statistics

Text Box: Myth: People who abuse are "crazy."

4) Knopp, F.H. (1984). *Retraining Adult Sex Offenders: Methods and Models.* Syracuse, NY: New York State Council of Churches.

Novak, B., McDermott, B.E., Scott, C.L., Guillory, S. (2007). Sex offenders and insanity: An examination of 42 individuals found not guilty by reason of insanity. *Journal of the American Academy of Psychiatry and Law Online* 35(4), 444-450. Retrieved November 20, 2008 from http://www.jaapl.org/cgi/content/full/35/4/444

Chapter 8: No, Really, I Need to Know, Why Does Abuse Happen?
Text Box: Myth: People who offend sexually are themselves past victims of sexual abuse.

1) Friedrich, W., Fisher, J.L., Dittner, C.A., Acton, R., Berliner, L., Butler, J., Damon, L., Davies, W.H., Grey, A., Wright, J. (2001). *Child sexual behavior inventory: Normative, psychiatric and sexual abuse comparisons.* Child Maltreatment, 6(1) 37-49.

Friedrich, W.N., Davies, W., Fehrer, E., & Wright, J. (2003). Sexual behavior problems in preteen children: Developmental, ecological, and behavioral correlates. *Annals of the New York Academy of Sciences,* 989, 95-104.

Hanson, R.K. (1991). *Characteristics of sex offenders who were abused as children.* In R. Langevin (Ed.), *Sexual offenders and their victims* (pp. 105-119). Oakville, Ontario: Juniper Press.

Kaufman, J & Ziegler, E. (1987). Do abused children become abused adults? *American Journal of Orthopsychiatry,* 57, 186-192.

Lambie, I., Seymour, F., Lee, A., & Adams, P. (2002). *Resiliency in the victim-offender cycle in male sexual abuse. Sexual Abuse: A Journal of Research and Treatment,* 14(1), 31-48.

Widom, C., & Ames, M. (1994). Criminal consequences of childhood sexual victimization. Child Abuse & Neglect, 18(4) 303-318.

Text Box: Shame

2) Jensen, A. (2006). *Discovering integrity: Working with shame without shaming young people who have abused.* In R.E. Longo & D.S. Prescott (Eds.), *Current perspectives: Working with sexually aggressive youth and youth with sexual behavior problems* (pp.119-141). Holyoke, MA: NEARI Press.

Text Box: The Difference Between Sexual Play and Sexual Abuse

3) Fathers' Guide to Parenting (July 7, 2008). *What is normal sexual play and behaviour in young children?* Retrieved November 24, 2008, from http://www.diyfather.com/content/What_is_normal_sexual_play_and_behaviour_in_young_children

Gil, E. & Johnson, T.C. (1993). *Sexualized Children.* New York: Launch.

James, B., & Nasjleti, M. (1989). *Treating sexually abused children and their families.* Palo Alto: Consulting Psychological Press, Inc.

Metsakis, A (1994). *The complete treatment of post traumatic stress disorder.* New York: Launch.

Chapter 9: Boundaries
Text Box: The Difference Between Sexual Play and Sexual Harassment

1) Berman, H., Straatman, A., Hunt, K., Izumi, J., & MacQuarrie, B. (2002). *Sexual harassment: The unacknowledged face of violence in the lives of girls.* In H. Berman and Y. Jiwani (Eds.), *In the best interests of the girl child* (pp. 15-44). London, ON: The Alliance of Five Research Centres on Violence.

Sexual harassment among youth. (n.d.). Retrieved July 13, 2008, from http://www.ucalgary.ca/resolve/violenceprevention/English/reviewprog/harassintro.htm

Chapter 12: Feeling Mixed Up
Text Box: Making A Comfort Box

1) Maltz, W. (2001). *Sexual healing journey: A guide for survivors of sexual abuse* (2nd ed.) pp 254-255 New York: Harper Collins Publishers.

Chapter 13: Bear
Text Box: Sex in Advertizing

1) Christakis, D.A., Zimmerman, E.J., DiGiuseppe, D.L., & McCarty, C.A. (2004). Early television exposure and subsequent attentional problems in children. *Pediatrics*, 113(4), 708-713.

Bushman, B.J., & Anderson, C.A. (2001) Media violence and the American public: Scientific facts versus media misinformation. *American Psychologist*, 56(6/7), 477-489.

Chapter 15: Trying To Relax
Text Box: A Few Common Feelings

1) Adapted from Mayer, A. 1990. *Child sexual abuse and the courts.* Holmes Beach, Florida: Learning Publications Inc.

Briere, J. & Elliot, D.M. (2003). Prevalence and psychological sequelae of self-reported childhood physical and sexual abuse in a general population sample of men and women. *Child Abuse & Neglect,* 27, 1205-1222.

Dube, S.R., Anda, R.F., Whitfield, C.L., Brown, D.W., Felitti, V.J., Dong, M. & Giles, W.H. (2005). Long term consequences of childhood sexual abuse by gender of victim. *American Journal of Preventative Medicine,* 28(5), 430-438.

Timms, R. & Connors, P. 1992. *Embodying healing: Integrating bodywork and psychotherapy in recovery from childhood sexual abuse.* Shoreham, Vermont: The Safer Society Press.

Text Box: Dealing with Big Feelings and Bad Memories

2) Najavitis, L.M. (2002). *Seeking safety: A treatment manual for PTSD and substance abuse.* p 133 New York: Guilford.

Chapter 16: Things to Do with Difficult Feelings
Text Box: Eating Disorders and Sexual Abuse

1) Ackard, D.M. & Neumark-Sztainer, D. (2002). Date violence and date rape among adolescents: Associations with disordered eating and psychological health. *Child Abuse & Neglect,* 26(5), 455-473.

Prendergast, W.E. (1993). *The merry-go-round of abuse: Identifying and treating survivors.* New York: Haworth.

Wonderlich, S.A., Crosby, R.D., Mitchell, J.E., Roberts, J.A., Haseltine, B., DeMuth, G. & Thompson, K. (2000). Relationship of childhood sexual abuse and eating disturbance in children. *Journal of the American Academy of Child and Adolescent Psychiatry* 39: 1277-1283.

Chapter 18: Jake
Text Box: Focusing on Your Heart

1) Inspired by the Heartmath Solution, Doc Childre and Howard Martin with Donna Beech. See www.heartmath.org for more information.

Chapter 19: What to Do if You Feel Like Hurting Yourself
Text Box: Substance Abuse and Sexual Abuse

1) Bulik, C.M., Prescott, C.A. & Kendler, K.S. (2001). Features of childhood sexual abuse and the development of psychiatric and substance use disorders. *The British Journal of Psychiatry,* 179, 444-449.

Critchlow (1983). Blaming the booze: The attribution of responsibility for drunken behavior. *Personality and Social Psychology Bulletin,* 23, 1574-1586.

Kendler, K.S., Bulik, C.M., Silberg, J., Hettema, J.M., Myers, J. & Prescott, C.A. (2000). Childhood sexual abuse and adult psychiatric and substance use disorders in women: An epidemiological and co-twin control analysis. *Archives of General Psychiatry* 57(10), 953-959.

Richardson, D. and Campbell, J.L. (1982). Alcohol and rape: The effect of alcohol on attributions of blame for rape. *Personality and Social Psychology Bulletin,* 8, 468-476.

Text Box: Substance Abuse and Sexual Abuse

2) Finkelhor, D. & Dziuba-Leatherman, J. (1994). *Children as victims of violence: A national survey.* Pediatrics, 94(4), 413-420.

Sartor, C.E., Agrawal, A., McCutcheon, V.V., Duncan, A.E. & Lynskey, M.T. (2008). Disentangling the complex association between childhood sexual abuse and alcohol-related problems: a review of methodological issues and approaches. *Journal for the Study of Alcohol & Drugs,* 69(5), 718-727.

Chapter 20: Tara and I Talk
Text Box: When You Feel Your Friend's Pain

1) V. Gordon (personal communication "pulling your feelings back with a magnet" concept, 2007).

Chapter 21: We Learn about Sticking Up for Ourselves
Text Box: What Are Your Absolutes

1) M. Krohn (personal communication "absolutes" concept, July 2007).

Chapter 24: Therapists Stink
Text Box: When Parents Get in Your Space

1) Love, P., & Robinson, J. (1990). The emotional incest syndrome: What to do when a parent's love rules your life. New York: Bantam.

Chapter 25: More Hard Things Happen to Tara and Me
Text Box: How Do You Feel about Your Body?

1) Adapted from: Bean, B. & Bennett, S. The Me Nobody Knows; A Guide for Teen Survivors (1993). New York, Macmillan, Inc.

Text Box: Imagine Holding Hands — How Do You Feel Before, During, After

2) Ibid..

Chapter 31: Changes
Text Box: What Are Your Personal Space Boundaries?

1) Adapted from Adams, C., & Fay, J. (1981). *No More Secrets,* pp 56-57. San Luis Obispo, California: Impact.

Text Box: Give Yourself a Butterfly Hug

2) B. Parrot, (personal conversation, The *"Butterfly Hug"* is an

EMDR technique, developed by Lucina Artigas, 2005). See also www.EMDRI.org.

Chapter 32: The Second to the Last Group
Text Box: Forgetting Painful Memories

1) Briere, J. & Conte, J. (1993). Self-reported amnesia in adults molested as children. *Journal of Traumatic Stress,* 6(1), 21-31.

Herman, J. & Schatzow, E. (1987). Recovery and verification of memories of childhood sexual trauma. *Psychoanalytical Psychology.* 4(1), 1-14.

Hopper, J. (September 27, 2008). Recovered memories of sexual abuse. Retrieved on November 24, 2008, from http://www.jimhopper.com/memory/.

Loftus, E.F. & Davis, D. (2006). Recovered memories. *Annual Review of Clinical Psychology,* 2, 469-498.

Williams, L.M. (1992). Adult memories of childhood abuse: Preliminary findings from a longitudinal study. *The Advisor.* Chicago, Illinois: APSAC.

Chapter 33: Trees
Text Box: How Will I Know When I Have Healed?

1) Adapted/derived from the work of Yvonne Dolan, Steve De Shazer and Ron Kral

Endnotes for "More Stuff"

1) When You Have to Go to Court

Mayer, A. (1990). *Child sexual abuse and the courts*. Holmes Beach, Florida: Learning Publications Inc.

National Center for Missing and Exploited Children. (1988). *Just in case…* Parental guidelines in case your child is testifying in court. (brochure).

Vukelic, J. (2005). Testifying under oath: *How to be an effective witness:* 41 tips to prepare you for court. Volcano, California: Volcano Press.

2) A Physical Exam

National Victim Center and National Crime Victims Research and Treatment Center (1992). *Rape in America: A report to the nation,* Arlington VA: Author.

3) Sex Offender Treatment Programs

("Studies show that some types of offences can be greatly reduced with therapy.")

Alexander, M. (1999). Sexual offender treatment efficacy. *Sexual Abuse: A Journal of Research and Treatment,* 11(2): 101-116.

Center for Sex Offender Management (August 2000). *Myths and facts about sex offenders*. Retrieved November 22, 2008, from http://www.csom.org/pubs/mythsfacts.html

Hanson, R.K., and Bussiere, M.T. (1998). Predicting relapse: A meta-analysis of sex offender recidivism studies. *Journal of Consulting Psychology,* 66(2), 348-362.
Nicholaichuk, T., Gordon, A., Gu, D., & Wong, S. (2000).

Outcome of an institutional sexual offender treatment program: A comparison between treated and matched untreated offenders. *Sexual Abuse: A Journal of Research and Treatment,* 12(2), 139-153.

Ward, T., & Stewart, C.A. (2003). Good lives and the rehabilitation of sexual offenders. In T. Ward, D.R. Lars & S.M. Hudson (Eds.), *Sexual Deviance: Issues and controversies* (pp 21-44). Thousand Oaks, CA: Sage.

4) Sex Offender Programs

("What type of offenses are more amenable to treatment?")

Aos, S., Miller, M., & Drake, E. (2006). Evidence-based adult correction programs: What works and what does not. Olympia, WA: *Washington State Institute for Public Policy.*

Bickley, J.A., & Beech, R. (2003). Implications for treatment of sexual offenders of the Ward and Hudson model of relapse. *Sexual Abuse: A Journal of Research and Treatment,* 15, 121-134.

Center for Sex Offender Management (August 2000). *Myths and facts about sex offenders.* Retrieved November 22, 2008, from http://www.csom.org/pubs/mythsfacts.html

Craissatic, J. & Beech, A. (2005). Risk prediction and failure in a complete urban sample of sex offenders. *Journal of Forensic Psychiatry and Psychology,* 16, 24-40.

Hanson, K. & Bussiere, M. (1998). Predicting relapse: a meta-analysis of sexual offender recidivism studies. *Journal of Consulting and Clinical Psychology,* 86, 348-362.

Hanson, K., & Harris, A.J.R. (2001). A structured approach to evaluating change among sexual offenders. *Sexual Abuse: A Journal of Research and Treatment,* 13, 105-122.

5) Is It Harder for Boys to Tell?

("[B]oys are most frequently abused by men, although reports of female abusers are increasing.")

Dube, S.R., Anda, R.F., Whitfield, C.L., Brown, D.W., Felitti, V.J., Dong, M. & Giles, W.H. (2005). Long term consequences of childhood sexual abuse by gender of victim. *American Journal of Preventative Medicine,* 28(5), 430-438

Finkelhor, D, Hotaling, G., Lewis, I.A., Smith, C. (1990). Sexual abuse in a national survey of adult men and women: Prevalence characteristics and risk factors. *Child Abuse and Neglect,* 19: 557-568.

Fritz, G.S., Stoll, K. & Wagner, N.A. (1981). A comparison of males and females who were sexually molested as children. *Journal of Sex and Marital Therapy,* 7, 54-59.

Green, A.H. (1999). Female sex offenders. In J.A. Shaw (Ed.), *Sexual Aggression,* (pp. 195-210). Washington D.C.: American Psychiatric Press.

Groth, A.N. & Oliveri, F. (1989). *Understanding sexual abuse behavior and differentiating among sexual abusers.* In S. Sgroi (Ed), Vulnerable Populations, Vol. 2, (pp. 309-327). Lexington, MA: Lexington Books. Holmes, W., & Slap, G. (1998). Sexual abuse of boys: Definition, prevalence, correlates, sequelae, and management. *Journal of the American Medical Association,* 280: 1855-1862.

Liask, D., Hooper, J., & Song, P. (1996). Factors in the cycle of violence: Gender rigidity and emotional constriction. *Journal of Traumatic Stress* 9: 721-743.

Vandiver, D.M. & Walker, J.T. (2002). Female sex offenders: An overview and analysis of 40 cases. *Criminal Justice Review,* 27, 284-300.

6) Is It Harder for Boys to Tell?
("[G]irls are more frequently abused than boys, and are more likely than boys to report sexual abuse.")

Finkelhor, D, Hotaling, G., Lewis, I.A., Smith, C. (1990). Sexual abuse in a national survey of adult men and women: Prevalence characteristics and risk factors. *Child Abuse and Neglect,* 19: 557-568.

Jewkes, R., Sen, P., & Garcia-Moreno, C. (2002) Sexual Violence. In E.Krug, L. Dalhberg, J.A. Mercy, A.B. Zwi, & R. Lozano, *World report of violence and health* (pp 147-181). Geneva, Switzerland: The World Health Organization.

7) Is it Harder for Boys to Tell?
"Boys are more likely to become physiologically aroused during an abuse situation, even when they are repulsed by what is happening."

Gartner, R.B. (1999). *Understanding sexual abuse behavior and differing among sexual abusers.* In Sgroi (Ed.), Vulnerable populations, Vol. 2, (pp. 309-327). Lexington, MA: Lexington Books

8) Is it Harder for Boys to Tell?
("They are also more likely to abuse alcohol and drugs and to be suicidal.")

Holmes, W.C. & Slap, G.B. (1998). Sexual abuse of boys: Definition, prevalence, sequelae, and management. *Journal of the American Medical Association,* 280(21): 1855-1872.

9) Sexual Abuse by Females
("According to current research, most of the time, the people who commit sexual abuse are male. But women and adolescent girls do abuse.")

Green, A.H. (1999). Female sex offenders. In J.A. Shaw (Ed.), *Sexual Aggression.* Washington D.C.: American Psychiatric Press.

Vandiver, D.M. & Walker, J.T. (2002). Female sex offenders: An overview and analysis of 40 cases. *Criminal Justice Review,* 27, 284-300.

10) Sexual Abuse by Females
(Number of people estimated abused by women)

Allen, J.G. (1996). Neurological basis of posttraumatic stress disorder: Implications for patient education and treatment. B*ulletin of the Menninger Clinic*, 60, 377-395.

We respectfully request that you inform us about any copyrighted materials that we inadvertently treated as in the public domain.

For Parents,

Therapists, and Other Adult Helpers

For Parents,

Therapists, and Other Adult Helpers

Introduction

Reading Abi's story in this book is one way that your child can begin to heal from sexual abuse. Even though both you and your child may want to avoid the subject, or think that it is best to simply put the past behind you, dealing with the thoughts and feelings about the abuse is the only way to truly move through it.

Sometimes the "fear of fear" has to be addressed before anything else can be dealt with. The fear of fear is what happens when a person is afraid to deal with something because she is afraid she will not be able to handle dealing with it. The idea of facing it is so overwhelming that this becomes the main issue and must be addressed first. It may even be your first issue to address.

Acknowledging that the abuse has deeply affected and changed you is important too. You may need some support to get through the feelings that both you and your child are experiencing. It can be helpful to have your own therapist or support system so that you can be fully available for your child when she needs you. If you are unable to hear her account of the abuse or to understand why she is acting the way she is, it will be nearly impossible for you to be able to provide a container for her feelings, which is what she needs from you.

The way that you respond to your child can be even more important in her healing process than the actual events of the abuse. Because of this reality, you will need to have some facts and information that sustain and nurture you. Unless you feel fed, it is impossible for you to nurture your child. And because the legal system can be so daunting (and at times unfriendly), you need an ally at your side who will help to promote real healing and not simply retribution.

While getting caught up in the legal battles or the need to punish the person who abused your child can be a piece of the process, it is not the support your child needs to heal. She needs to know that you are by her side and able to promote her growth and movement as she works through very difficult feelings. If you have a place to vent, scream, and cry, you can get your own support and then be the person who can tolerate all of those same things from your child, rather than meeting your needs at her expense.

Many parents ask, "Why didn't she tell me sooner?" The reality is that only one in ten abused children report their sexual abuse at all.[11] Delayed disclosure or no disclosure at all is most frequently seen in younger victims, and in victims who know their perpetrators. The likelihood that a child will disclose is increased when the perpetrator is a stranger or if life threat or physical injury is involved.[12] It is practically magical that your child was able to trust someone enough to tell at all, or simply miraculous that the abuse was discovered in some other way. Telling about sexual abuse is so difficult that almost no one does it. By talking to you about her abuse, she has trusted you with something very deep and scary.

A few other things to keep in mind include being aware of anniversary dates (such as the birthday of an abusing relative, a day the abuse escalated, disclosure day, the date of her testimony in court, the date of the verdict and/or sentencing, and other dates that you may or may not be aware of) which are annual reminders of traumatic events. These are times that your child may feel overwhelmed or act out, become more testy, depressed or aggressive. Some people become suicidal around anniversary dates. Usually your child will have no understanding or recognition that she is reacting to an anniversary, and even if she does, it is unlikely that she will understand why. Current losses or changes in friendships, residence, or schools, can also be difficult, and remind her of less concrete and frequently unacknowledged losses, such as the loss of innocence, the loss of dignity, or the loss of belief in herself.

Children often go through stages of healing. She may need extra support, or experience strong or confusing feelings, thoughts, and beliefs, as she goes through different developmental periods. Developmental milestones, such as a first date, the first time a person chooses to have sex, beginning menses, marriage, pregnancy, child birth, and when the child(ren) of the now-adult survivor reaches the age at which she herself was abused are times that you may see increased feelings of fear, rage, confusion, or depression, and a need for increased care and support. Many therapists employ an "open door" policy in order to account for the need for this type of periodic support.

Don't fall into the trap of believing that child sexual abuse is so painful and devastating that it is forever damaging and she can never heal. This belief will serve only to keep her stuck and delay or derail her healing. Your support through this healing process may well help her mature into an adult with especially clear wisdom and compassion for herself and others.

Keep the lines of communication open, even if it means you are the only one talking. Remember, if it's a forbidden subject it's secret, if it's secret it can be hidden. Balance this knowledge with your child's need to move at her own pace and not be questioned incessantly.

Developing a same-sex sexual orientation is sometimes believed to be "caused" by being abused, however, that opinion is not based in fact. Some children who are already aware of their sexual orientation may in fact find it more difficult to disclose sexual abuse because they are frightened that this will be discovered and not accepted, or discovered and blamed on the abuse. Many young people experiment and have questions about being gay or straight or somewhere in between. A sexual abuse survivor may have more questions and feel more frequently confused about sexuality, but this is normal. For additional resources on sexual orientation, see the resource list included. Whatever sexual identity your child is experimenting with, or questioning, it is important that you support her, even if you cannot embrace her choices.

Above all, take care of yourself. You cannot be available for anyone else if you are depleted. Be gentle with yourself. This is a difficult and grueling situation to have to go through. You will undoubtedly make some mistakes. Apologize and move on. This will be difficult, but you can make it through!

Kimber & PeggyEllen

If You Have Your Own History of Sexual Abuse as a Child

If you are the parent of a child who has been sexually abused and you have your own history of sexual abuse, you may be experiencing many confusing feelings. Especially if you have never told anyone about your sexual abuse, you may be having strong or overwhelming emotions. You may even start to feel like you are going crazy.

This isn't unusual. In fact, when you have locked away such memories, and then are reminded of painful events, it is common to begin to have small glimpses of those memories, feelings in your body, strange dreams, and new fears. You might notice shadows out of the corner of your eye, feel as though things seem "unreal" or as if you are not fully "in" your body.

One of the reasons that these feelings and sensations are so powerful and seem so crazy-making, is that you are thinking about them with your adult mind, but feeling them in a child state: the age at which you were abused, told about the abuse, or started to heal.

Imagery-based therapies, like Eye Movement Desensitization and Reprocessing (EMDR), and Internal Family Systems Therapy (IFS), can help you to reprocess these memories on an emotional and intellectual level, as well as beginning to integrate the body-mind connection. Therapies such as these will allow you to remember events the same way you always have, but to feel significantly differently about them. Working through these memories will mean that they no longer have power over you, but that you have power over them. When you have power over when and where and for how long you think about a painful experience, you will no longer feel as if you are going crazy.

If you are having powerful angry, depressed, or anxious feelings, please seek your own support and therapy so that you too can move through this painful experience and heal.

For a Resource List of books and websites please go to **www.neari.com/press** and look under the book's title "The Thursday Group."

What Should I Do When a Child Tells Me She Was Sexually Abused?

Believe the child.

It's important to believe a person who is telling you that they were abused. It is extremely rare for kids to lie about that abuse. In fact, less than 4 percent of all reports are false, and that is usually because an adult coached the child to lie, not because the child herself made up the abuse story. Children only fabricate abuse stories one half of one percent of the time. [13]

Don't make promises you can't keep.

While it may feel comforting and powerful to say, "This will never happen to you again," or "He's going to jail now and you'll never have to see him again," those are things that you have little or no control over. And if you make a promise you can't keep, it is you with whom the child will be angry, and you by whom the child will feel betrayed.

Be honest.

While everyone hopes it is so, it is not really truthful to tell a child, "This will all be over soon." Courts and legal processes are known to drag on, with hearings rescheduled and dates changed. And healing may be a lengthy process, too, with a period of intense therapy and emotional work, and breaks from dealing with it, then returns to therapy as new issues come up. The truth is that this may take a long time.

What can I say?

It took a lot of courage for you to tell me.

I'm going to find someone who can help you.

It's not your fault.

I'm sorry this happened to you.

You were very smart to tell.

You were very brave to tell.

I know it's not easy to talk about.

There are people we have to tell so that we can stop this from happening again.

What can I do?

Get down on the child's eye level.

Let the child talk at her own pace, don't rush things.

Allow the child to stop talking when she becomes uncomfortable.

Nod your head or say uh-huh, mmmm.

Listen a lot, talk a little.

Don't interpret, guess at what happened, or put words in the child's mouth.

Don't ask yes/no questions or 'why' questions.

Ask "how", "what", "when", and "where" questions instead.

Let the child use their own language, especially for body parts.

Try to be calm during the disclosure.

Be calm and still honest about your feelings in a way that lets the child know that she is not responsible for the abuse. Try not to allow your feelings to become bigger, more out of control, or more important than the child who is telling you about the abuse. Hold onto those strong feelings to vent with another adult at a different time. The child will need you to be able to provide her with the space to have her own feelings. If your feelings are bigger, seem stronger or more powerful, it leaves too little room for her to express her own feelings. This will result in the child shutting down and telling you less and less over time, or even recanting (saying that the abuse never happened).

Don't overemphasize the negative.

It can be particularly harmful to a child to suggest that the abuse will have life-long or damaging effects, or that it will alter the way she interacts with others. Although such outcomes are possible, it is also possible that the child will heal relatively quickly, or not need to "heal" at all. Sometimes we believe what we hear and then we create our reality from that (if I believe I am damaged for life I will be).

Everyone responds to abuse differently.

Some people can deal with abuse more quickly or fully than other people can. Not everyone requires therapy to deal with abusive situations. Kids who are acting out, appear anxious or depressed, or are hurting themselves or acting aggressive toward others should be evaluated for therapeutic services. You may want to wait and see if she is able to work through things on her own, or to "grow out of it", but remember, the sooner she receives help, the less likely she is to hurt herself or others, or to sustain long-term consequences from the abuse.

Give the child room to heal.

It may be hard to figure out when and how to talk about the abuse. If a child senses that you are uncomfortable, she will not talk to you about the abuse. On the other hand, bringing the abuse up all the time can prevent her from working through it in her own time. Simply giving her permission to talk about it when she is ready can do wonders for helping her feel comfortable and safe. If you are feeling confused about how to talk to a child about abuse, or feel the need to ask her repeated questions about the abuse, seek professional help from a therapist.

Parent Activities to Support Healing[14]

Your child may (or may not) regress to an earlier stage of emotional development during therapy because of the amount of emotional material being processed. She may act out more for a while or even behave disrespectfully toward you. You can help the most by being aware of this process and not expecting positive changes within the first few sessions, even though you may be disappointed and feel tempted to prematurely take your child out of therapy. Discontinuing therapy when your child is acting out or regressing may cause your child to feel unsafe and to regress even more, begin hurting herself, or withdraw.

After each session, your child will very likely need some extra support. The type of support can vary and is different for each child. You know your child best and will best be able to determine if she needs some quiet alone time, some quiet snuggle or reading time with you, or time to discharge energy by doing something active. Below are some ideas to help you to plan activities throughout the week between sessions. It is wise to plan something for directly after each therapy session as well. This can be something exciting and invigorating, like a run on the beach, something connecting, like eating a snack alone with you, or something quiet, like some alone time in her tree house. The activity will depend on your individual child, and may change based on the particular therapy session or the child's mood.

For Younger Elementary School-Aged Children:

Play baby games like Peek-a-Boo, Hide and Seek, and Patty-Cake. It may seem silly given your child's age, but with the emotion-laden content of material being released, it is typical for children to need some extra care and for them to act in a manner below their chronological age.

Provide lots of gentle touch, such as a big hug, a back massage, or a roll on the floor.

Try not to engage in active touch, such as tickling games, right at first. Expressing feelings through the body is sometimes painful and may be too much for the child during her healing process. The adrenaline that active touch stimulates may be too close to the adrenaline she experienced during abuse, causing her to have feelings and behaviors that neither of you is likely to understand (such as explosive anger, hitting you without thinking, screaming, intense fear, or crying uncontrollably). Once your child has worked through some of her feelings about touch, she will be more able to accept different types of touching. For now, it will be important to give her some space.

Get in rhythm with your child by using any song or rhyme paired with rocking, bouncing, or clapping. Substitute your child's name in songs and rhymes whenever possible. This can include songs and rhymes typically sung to very young children. Although she may think it is silly, it is really helping to reprogram her brain in a soothing manner.

Use sensory-based activities as a way of integrating the emotions being discharged with body memory. Any kind of clapping, drumming, or dance can help with integration. You can also play slippery hand games with lotion, give a hand or foot massage, or stack your hands alternating with your child's, pulling out the bottom one to put on top.

Snuggle while reading bedtime stories.

Rock and sing lullabies while cradling your child.

Brush her hair gently.

Snuggle next to her in bed at bedtime and tell each other the best and worst things that have happened that day. Have this sort of conversation at dinnertime if the snuggling is not accepted right now or if the content is too overwhelming at night.

"Paint" your child's face with your finger, pointing out each feature.

Tell your child the story of her birth or arrival into your family.

Cradle your child's face in your hands and tell how much you treasure him/her.

Spend extra time and kisses tucking your child in at night, especially on days when there has been conflict. The tuck-in time sets the stage for the next 8-12 hours of dreams and may also dictate the type of mood she is in when she wakes as well as how well she sleeps during the night.

For Older Children and Teens:

Even though some of the ideas listed above might seem childish or more appropriate for younger children, many can be used as-is or adapted for older children and teens. One of the things that happens to people who are healing from sexual abuse, is a need to act and be treated as younger than their chronological age. Re-doing some of the things you did with your child as an infant to re-create the attachment bond is important as a healing tool to reprogram brain pathways and reinforce a belief in love, safety, and self-esteem.

Other things that might prove helpful for teens and pre-teens include quiet walks together, attending a yoga or meditation class with your child, taking turns massaging one another's hands or feet, listening to the music your child loves and discussing the meaning of the lyrics, and simply eating a quiet or silent meal together.

Reading books or stories that hold strong metaphors of healing (such as Clarisa Pinkola Este's stories, or "The Tree that Survived the Winter" by Mary Fahy) can also be inspiring and uplifting, without ever having to directly talk about the sexual abuse. Resist pointing out the connections between the stories and the child's experience, and instead allow her to make her own connections in time, as she is ready.

Tips for Dads of Adolescent Girls

Being the father of an adolescent girl is difficult under the best of circumstances. Your daughter is struggling with the transition from childhood to young adulthood, and you probably are too.

Developing breasts can get in the way of "tomboy" activities that girls may have previously enjoyed with their fathers, and they become noticeable when hugging dad too. Dads may back completely away from physical contact with their daughters, or try to maintain a physical closeness, but feel uncomfortable when doing so.

Many fathers begin to feel an uncomfortable tension as their daughters mature sexually. Feeling this tension does not mean that there is something wrong with you or that you are going to act on those feelings. However, if the feelings are more than fleeting, bother you, or get in the way of your relationship, you may want to get a reality check from a knowledgeable therapist. If you are afraid that you will act on your thoughts or feelings, or if you have acted on your feelings by being inappropriate with your daughter sexually, you must seek help. Your own sense of self-respect requires it and your daughter deserves it.

What Can We as a Society Do to Stop Abuse From Happening?

We need to hear the evil, see the evil, and speak the evil. In other words, we must believe that it is true and do something about it. For too long, we have denied that abuse happens, and we have allowed children and adults to suffer because of our fears of seeing what is really happening, and because of our strong need to believe that it isn't happening. It is time to see what is right in front of us and to do something about it. Less than 4 percent of all disclosures of abuse are false reports.[15] And perhaps 80 to 90 percent of abuse never even gets reported.[16] When we believe children they will feel strong and powerful and protected.

Teach sex education and healthy body awareness. When our children understand their bodies, and are taught to honor and respect bodies of all shapes and sizes, then they will feel strong and powerful and they will be more likely to tell a parent, friend, or ally if someone tries to harm them. Avoid scaring your children with "stranger danger" or other scare tactics; instead make this a part of other "safety" talks you have with your children, such as water safety, road safety, etc.

Learn about sexual abuse, how to identify it, and how to prevent it. Darkness to Light (see www.Darkness2Light.org) has a great curriculum that teaches adults that it is their job to protect children, rather than the child's job to learn how to say "no" and "tell someone."

We still need to teach our children that they have the right to say "no" and how to say it. If our children are taught how to protect themselves then they will feel stronger and more powerful, and will walk tall and speak forcefully. Teaching children such skills is important, but they do not reduce our responsibility as adults to protect children from harm. Unfortunately, we must also teach children that we recognize that there are some adults that will ignore children when they say no, and that this is not their fault.

Don't encourage children to hug or kiss someone if they do not feel like doing so. We often ask children to "Hug Aunt Matilda" or "Kiss your Uncle Jared," when we wouldn't dream of instructing an adult to do such a thing. Our intention is usually to teach good manners and relationship connections, but children need to know that we will respect their desire to not be affectionate at any given moment.

Establish safety rules in our homes, schools and communities. Policies that protect children are necessary and they will speak volumes about how we feel about children and will help them to feel strong and powerful.

Even more powerful is modeling respect for children as discrete, temporarily dependent but autonomous individuals. If you listen carefully and attentively and believe children in everyday things, they are more likely to trust that you will listen carefully and believe them when it's as important and scary as disclosing sexual abuse.

Adults need to help kids make a plan for who to tell, where to go, and how to handle abuse if it does happen. This preparation is like having a fire drill at school or a family escape plan for fires or other destructive emergencies at home: you hope it will never happen, but you want your child to know what to do, just in case it does. If you know how you will deal with something before it happens, it has less power over you, and you will be able to take charge, feel strong and powerful, and get help.

Value all people, and emphasize the importance of children. When we devalue someone we devalue everyone. We cannot empower a child while putting someone else down.

Be "askable." Encourage children to ask questions and to talk about sex and sexuality. As long as sex, sexuality, and body parts are something normal and natural to talk about, there is no stigma, and therefore, no shame. If it is an uncomfortable or forbidden subject, kids don't know how to talk about it, or how to tell if someone engages them sexually. Talking about it will reduce shame, isolation and loneliness and will help to prevent problems later.

Support other people who have been hurt or abused. Donate money to agencies that support victims of sexual abuse. Volunteer your time working with survivors. Learn more about what you can do to help spread the message and teach people about sexual abuse. Silence is powerful and necessary for an offender to succeed. If we refuse to be silent then the abuse will have to stop. It won't happen overnight, but it will happen.

Support providing treatment for people who have sexually offended. As much as you may want awful things to happen to the person who abused your loved one, punishment will not stop abuse from happening. And offenders do eventually get out of prison, either with the tools and skills to change their behaviors or without them. There are good statistics that indicate that appropriate treatment really can work for some people who offend sexually.[17] When people who abuse get the help they need to stop hurting people it will help all of us to be safe and empowered.

Don't ignore your inner voice; if you think something feels wrong, check it out! You're probably right and you deserve to believe in yourself.

Sometimes I want to say, "Hey people, get a clue." Abi

Some Facts about Rape

In legal terms, rape is one type of sexual assault.

Six out of 10 sexual assaults occur in the home of the victim or in the home of a friend, neighbor, or relative.[18]

One-third of all sexual assault victims are under the age of twelve.[19]

More than half of all rape victims have been sexually assaulted more than once.[20]

Victims of sexual assault are more likely to develop Post Traumatic Stress Disorder or Major Depression, and to attempt suicide than people who have not been abused.[21]

Only one in ten rapes is reported.

Rape is the most underreported of all major crimes.

Rape includes any type of forced penetration of the vagina or anus.

Types of Therapy That May Be Helpful in Healing From Abuse
And Other Types of Trauma

 Talk Therapy: The therapist helps you find your own strengths and gives you support to identify and work with your feelings. You can talk about the abuse and how it has affected you. Together you can look at your beliefs about the abuse, and sort through any misunderstandings. Talk therapy is often used with other types of therapy such as art therapy and skills training.

 Family Therapy: One goal of therapy is to help the person who has been abused to understand the abuse as something that was done to her, not something that defines who she is. Because we get a lot of our ideas about who we are from the families that we live in, it may be important to include other family members, especially parents, in therapy. Family therapy is not appropriate for everyone, especially not in families where there isn't enough safety or protection for the abused person. Family therapy can be difficult, but it is also very rewarding, and often leaves family members feeling closer, safer, and better able to communicate with one another.

 Group Therapy: There are different types of group therapy. Some groups, like the one in this book, are more about education. Others are more process-oriented and work much like individual therapy that simply involves a lot of other people, thus reducing the feelings of isolation and differentness. Group therapy usually lasts 6-12 weeks, and typically includes people who are of similar age and who have gone through similar experiences.

Expressive Arts Therapy: The therapist has paints, clay, markers or other art supplies that can be used to express feelings and describe situations. Sometimes an art therapist will ask you to do some specific kind of art. Other times, you get to choose what you create. Most art therapists don't "interpret" or try to guess what you are saying through the art. Just the expression of feelings through art is in itself healing.

 Play Therapy: Play therapy helps with expressing feelings and making positive connections in your nervous system. It's a way of talking without using words and helps process those experiences that may be too powerful for words. You use toys, a sand tray with figurines, puppets, a doll house, and other things that help to express your feelings (just through play!). It can also help you access your fun side and experience joy again.

 Skills Training: The focus of skills training (sometimes called activity therapy) is on learning new behaviors. You may practice relaxing, speaking up for yourself, meditation, or coping with difficult feelings. Sometimes the practice is with other people in a group or community setting.

 Desensitization Training: The purpose of this technique is to take the emotional charge out of the memories of the abuse and things that remind you of the abuse. Using relaxation exercises and body awareness, you learn to stay relaxed even when you have memories of the abuse. EMDR (Eye Movement Desensitization and Reprocessing) is a kind of desensitization training that uses talk and movement therapy in a specialized way.

Energy Healing: Electromagnetic energy moves through and around our bodies. We use this energy for many things including moving our muscles, and thinking. Abuse and fear can cause constriction and blocks in our energy. The energy healer works with patterns of energy moving in and around your body. She or he can help you to release blocks and constrictions. Some energy healers do "hands-on" work. Others work without touching you. You keep your clothes on during the healing.

Therapy combinations: Some therapists combine several different types of therapy when they are working with an individual; for example, talk therapy and play or art therapy, or family therapy and individual therapy. There are many kinds of therapy. It is not necessary to use all of them to heal. Use those with which you feel comfortable and those that are available to you. Your therapist will probably have some recommendations as well.

Body Work

In addition to the therapies listed above, body work can be particularly helpful in the healing process. Body work can release tensions and feelings from the abuse that have become locked in your muscles and other body tissues. It helps to ground you in your body and to increase your comfort level with your own body.

Because the therapist may be touching you, it is especially important that you feel safe. The therapist must be willing to stop immediately if at any point you request it. If you don't feel safe, the body work is not going to be helpful.

Body work can bring up strong emotions, so it's a good idea to think about the timing before starting this type of work. Body work is something that you may choose to do after you have been in therapy for a while and both you and your therapist (and your parents) feel that you are ready to do some more work. Body therapy can bring up memories or feelings that you have stored in your body, but do not necessarily remember in your brain. Having a skilled and knowledgeable body therapist is important because even body work that is not specifically meant to deal with the sexual abuse can bring up strong emotions. Cranial sacral therapy and yoga are thought to be two excellent body therapies for healing from sexual abuse. Several other options are listed below. Some kinds of body work may be easier for you to tolerate than others. Honor yourself by not forcing yourself into something you aren't ready for.

Cranial Sacral Therapy: Using gentle touch, the therapist helps your body let go of tension around the bones and ligaments of your spinal column, neck, and skull, so that the fluids bathing your brain and the nerves of your spinal column can move in their normal slow wave patterns. The client generally lies on a massage table wearing comfortable clothing.

Yoga: A system of stretching and breathing positions that can help people become more aware of their bodies. It is calming and centering. Usually yoga classes have an instructor who leads a group of students in the various positions. People wear comfortable stretchy clothing.

Movement Therapy: Our growing bodies need to feel safe so that nerve connections can take place in a healthy way throughout our bodies. Movement therapy can allow your body to release hurtful memories and make nerve connections you may have missed because of fear. There are many types of movement therapy. The therapist may use aids such as balls, scarves, or music, to help you move your body in new ways and become aware of textures and pressure. You may be taught special exercises that help your body experience easier ways of breathing or moving. Dance, yoga, Feldenkrais, Cortical Reeducation, Eutony, the Alexander Technique, Body-Mind Centering, Tai Chi, and martial arts are all types of movement therapy. Some kinds are exploratory and playful. Others involve structured exercises. You will need to wear loose-fitting, comfortable clothes.

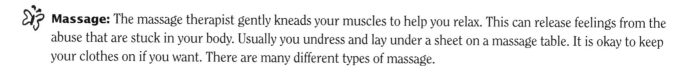

Massage: The massage therapist gently kneads your muscles to help you relax. This can release feelings from the abuse that are stuck in your body. Usually you undress and lay under a sheet on a massage table. It is okay to keep your clothes on if you want. There are many different types of massage.

Rolfing or Structural Integration: The practitioner, or Rolfer, uses his or her hands to deeply move your muscles and tissues. Like massage, this can release feelings from the abuse that are stuck in your body tissues. You usually lie on a massage table in your underwear.

Karate: This is an excellent type of martial art body work that teaches a person to have control over her own body, to understand how her body works, to make her body move in a way that feels strong and powerful, and to know in her muscle memory and her mind that she can defend herself if she needs to.

Other types: There are many types of body work. Make sure both you and your parents or guardians are comfortable with the person providing the treatment. Your therapist or case manager should be a part of the process too, so that all the people who are helping you to heal know what all the other people who are helping you are doing. This reduces the possibility of people doing different things that may be at cross-purposes to each other, or of overloading your system in a way that could delay your healing.

Endnotes for Parents, Therapists and Other Helpers

11) Introduction for Parents and Professionals
("Only one in ten children report sexual abuse at all.")

Darkness to Light (n.d.). Statistics surrounding child sexual abuse. Retrieved November 24, 2008, from http://www.darkness2light.org/KnowAbout/statistics_ 2.asp.

National Victim Center and National Crime Victims Research and Treatment Center (1992). Rape in America: A report to the nation, Arlington VA: Author.

12) Introduction for Parents and Professionals
("Likelihood that a disclosure will happen is increased if the perpetrator is a stranger or if life threat or physical injury is involved.")

Hanson, R.F., Resnick, H.S., Saunders, B.E., Kilpatrick, D.G., & Best, C. (1999). Factors related to reporting of childhood rape. Child Abuse & Neglect, 23, 559-569.

13) What Should I Do When a Child Tells Me She Was Sexually Abused? ("Less than 4 percent of all reports are false reports.")

Darkness to Light (n.d.). Statistics surrounding child sexual abuse. Retrieved November 24, 2008, from http://www.darkness2light.org/KnowAbout/statistics_2.asp.

Finkelhor. (1992). *Parent to parent: Talking to your children about preventing child sexual abuse.* VHS.

Goodwin, J. (1985). *Sexual abuse: Incest victims and their families.* Palo Alto, CA: Consulting Psychologists Press.

14) Parent Activities to Support Healing

Adapted from Bass, D. & Davis, L. (1994). *Helping them heal* (3rd Ed.): A guide for women survivors of childhood sexual abuse. Santa Cruz, California: Harper & Row Publishers.

15) What Can We as a Society Do to Stop Abuse from Happening? ("Less than 4 percent of all reports are false.")

Darkness to Light (n.d.). Statistics surrounding child sexual abuse. Retrieved November 24, 2008, from http://www.darkness2light.org/KnowAbout/statistics_2.asp.

Finkelhor. (1992). *Parent to parent: Talking to your children about preventing child sexual abuse.* VHS (available from produced by?).

Goodwin, J. (1985). Sexual abuse: incest victims and their families. Palo Alto: Consulting Psychologists Press, Inc.

16) **What Can We as a Society Do to Stop Abuse from Happening?** ("80-90 percent of abuse never gets reported.")

Darkness to Light (n.d.). *Statistics surrounding child sexual abuse.* Retrieved November 24, 2008, from http://www.darkness2light.org/KnowAbout/statistics_2.asp.

National Victim Center and National Crime Victims Research and Treatment Center (1992). *Rape in America: A report to the nation,* Arlington VA: Author.

17) *What Can We as a Society Do to Stop Abuse from Happening?* *("Treatment can help offenders.")*

Center for Sex Offender Management (August 2000). Myths and facts about sex offenders. Retrieved November 22, 2008, from http://www.csom.org/pubs/mythsfacts.html

Gretton, H.M., Catchpole, R.E.H., McBraie, M, Hare, R.D., & Reagan, K.V. (2005). The relationship between psychopathology, treatment completion, and criminal outcome over ten years: A study of adolescent sexual offenders. In M. Caldwell (Ed.), *Children and young people who sexually abuse: New theory, research, and practice developments* (pp. 19-31). London: Russell House.

18) **Some Facts about Rape** ("Six out of 10 sexual assaults occur in the home of the victim or in the home of a friend, neighbor, or relative .")

Center for Sex Offender Management (August 2000). *Myths and facts about sex offenders.* Retrieved November 22, 2008, from http://www.csom.org/pubs/mythsfacts.html

Greenfield, L. (1997). *Sex offenses and offenders: An analysis of data on rape and sexual assault.* Washington, DC: US Dept of Justice, Bureau of Justice Statistics

19) *Some Facts about Rape* *("One-third of all sexual assault victims are under the age of 12.")*

Darkness to Light (n.d.). Statistics surrounding child sexual abuse. Retrieved November 24, 2008, from http://www.darkness2light.org/KnowAbout/statistics_2.asp. Snyder, H.N. & Sickmund, M. (1999). *Juvenile Offenders and Victims: 1999 National Report.* Pittsburgh, PA: National Center for Juvenile Justice.

20) Some Facts about Rape
("More than half of rape victims have been raped more than once.")

Messman-Moore, T.L. & Long, P.J. (2000). Child sexual abuse and revictimization in the form of adult sexual abuse, adult physical abuse, and adult psychological maltreatment. *Journal of Interpersonal Violence,* 15(5), 489-502.

National Victim Center and National Crime Victims Research and Treatment Center (1992). *Rape in America: A report to the nation,* Arlington VA: Author.

21) Some Facts about Rape
("Victims of sexual assault are more likely to develop Post Traumatic Stress Disorder, Major Depression, and more likely to attempt suicide than people who have not been abused.")

Bulik, C.M., Prescott, C.A. & Kendler, K.S. (2001). Features of childhood sexual abuse and the development of psychiatric and substance use disorders. *The British Journal of Psychiatry,* 179, 444-449.
National Victim Center and National Crime Victims Research and Treatment Center (1992). *Rape in America: A report to the nation,* Arlington VA: Author.

Widom, C.S. (1999). Posttraumatic stress disorder in abused and neglected children grown up. *American Journal of Psychiatry,* 156(8), 1223-1229.

We respectfully request that you inform us about any copyrighted materials that we inadvertently treated as in the public domain.

Bibliography

Clarke, J.F. (Ed.). *A Gathering of Wisdoms: Tribal Mental Health: A Cultural Perspective* (1991). LaConner, WA: Swinomish Indian Tribal Community.

Darkness to Light (2003). *7 Steps to Protecting Our Children* (brochure).

National Committee for the Prevention of Child Abuse (n.d.). Scared Silent (brochure).

Black, C.A. & DeBlassie, R.R. (1993). *Sexual abuse in male children and adolescents: Indicators, effects, and treatments.* Adolescence, 28, 123-133.

Blanchard, G. (1998). *The difficult connection: The therapeutic relationship in sex offender treatment* (Rev. ed.). Brandon, VT: Safer Society Press.

Bolby, JA (1988). *A secure base: Parent-child attachment and healthy human development.* New York: Basic Books.

Bonner, B.L., Walker, C.E., & Berliner, L. (1999). *Children with sexual behavior problems: Assessment and treatment. National Center on Child Abuse and Neglect, Administration of Children, Youth, and Families,* U.S. Department of Health and Human Service.

Darves-Boronoz, J.M., Choquet, M., Ledoux, S., & Manifredi, R. (1998). Gender differences in symptoms of adolescents reporting sexual assault. *Social Psychiatry & Psychiatric Epidemiology,* 33, 111-117.

Evensen, K. (2007). *Pathway to hope: healing child sexual abuse video guidebook.* Washington, D.C.: U.S. Department of Justice, Office for Victims of Crime.

Gilgun, Jane F. (2006). *Children and adolescents with problematic sexual behaviors: Lessons from research on resilience.* In R.E. Longo & D.S. Prescott (Eds.). Current perspectives on working with sexually aggressive youth and youth with sexual behavior problems. (pp. 383-394). Holyoke, MA: Neari Press.

Levine, P.A. (1997). *Waking the tiger: Healing trauma:*

The innate capacity to transform overwhelming experiences. Berkeley, CA: North Atlantic Books.

Morrissette, P.J. (1991). The therapeutic dilemma with Canadian Native youth in residential care. *Child and Adolescent Social Work Journal,* 8(2), 89-99.

Napoleon, H. (1991). *Yuuyaraq: The way of the human being.* Fairbanks, AK: University of Alaska, Center for Cross Cultural Studies.

Rodenhauser, P. (1994). Cultural barriers to mental health care delivery. Alaska. *Journal of Mental Health Administration,* 21(1), 60-70.

Rothschild, B. (2000). *The body remembers: the psychophysiology of trauma and trauma treatment.* New York: Norton.

Ryan, G., & Lane, S. (1997). *Juvenile sexual offenders: Causes, consequences and correction* (Rev. ed.). San Francisco, CA: Jossey-Bass.

Salter, A. (2003). *Predators: pedophiles, rapists, and other sex offenders: Who they are, how they operate, and how we can protect our children.* New York: Basic Books.

Sgroi, S.M. (1982). *Handbook of clinical intervention in child sexual abuse.* New York: Haworth.

Snyder, H.N. (2000). *Sexual Assaults of young children as reported to law enforcement: Victim, incident, and offender characteristics.* Washington, D.C.: Bureau of Justice Statistics.

Stien, P.T., & Kendall, J.C. (2004). *Psychological trauma and the developing brain: neurologically based interventions for troubled children.* New York: Haworth.

Van der Kolk, B.A., McFarlane, A.C. & Weisaeth, L. (Eds.). (1996). *Traumatic stress: The effects of overwhelming experience on mind, body, and society.* New York: Guilford.

Glossary

Abuse: A bigger, older or more powerful person hurts or uses a younger or less powerful person. The abuser is trying to control the other person and/or to meet their own needs while ignoring the child's needs. Child abuse is against the law.

Anus: The opening in a person's bottom where feces (poop) comes out.

Anxiety: Extreme and constant worry about one or a number of things that result in the person not being able to function well in their day to day activities.

Bisexual: A person who is attracted sexually to both males and females.

Civil Court: The court that people go to if they are suing another person or a company for money. "Plaintiffs" (the persons suing) and "defendants" (the persons being sued) and their lawyers make their case against each other. There is no state prosecutor involved.

Clitoris: In a female, the tiny special organ that becomes hard and enlarged when the girl or woman is feeling sexual. It is located at the top of the opening of the vagina.

Criminal Court: Where adults must go when they are charged with a crime or when they are witnesses in a criminal case. The prosecutor (the lawyer representing the state) or "State's Attorney" or "District Attorney" presents the facts of the case based on evidence collected by law enforcement. The defendant, through his or her lawyer, has the opportunity to question or challenge the state's evidence, including witnesses, and to present evidence or witnesses that he or she did not commit the crime.

Defendant or Accused: A person accused of committing a crime who is required to go before a criminal court judge, at pre-trial hearings and/or at trial.

Defense Attorney: A lawyer who will be defending the person accused of sexually abusing you. This lawyer's job is to convince the judge and/or the jury that the person accused of abusing you is not guilty because you misunderstood, or it was someone else, or you imagined it. He or she will try to keep the defendant out of prison, even if the defendant is found guilty. He or she is working for the defendant.

Depression: An extreme feeling of sadness and loneliness that includes feelings of hopelessness and helplessness. Can include self-harm, suicidal thoughts, feelings, and attempts.

Elder: In many Alaska Native and American Indian cultures, respected individuals who have both aged past 50 or 60 years, and who have lived a life that has been respectful of the land, culture, and other individuals, are considered "Elders." An Elder holds certain traditional and valued knowledge, beliefs, and values which he or she passes on to younger generations. A true Elder does not abuse children.

Emotional Abuse: When someone scares a child or less powerful person, or tries to damage their self-confidence and self-esteem. This is done in order to control or punish the child or make themselves feel better at their victim's expense. A parent using emotional abuse might tell his/her kids that they are stupid, evil, or bad. He/she might threaten to hurt a child, to stop loving them, or leave them. He/she might expose them to things that they cannot handle or cope with. Sometimes one of several children in a family is singled out for abuse. Some types of emotional abuse are against the law.

Family Court: Where parents or adolescents go if they are accused of mistreating or abusing their children or younger brothers and sisters, or if they are victims or witnesses to such abuse within the family.

Flashback: When a person experiences the physical, visual, and auditory sensations of a traumatic event as if it were occurring in the present. When a person is having a flashback, they literally do not know that they are safe in the present moment. Instead, their mind and body tell them that the traumatic event is presently occurring even though it may have been months or even years since the actual event happened. Not all victims or survivors of trauma experience flashbacks.

Genitals: The sexual parts of our bodies between our legs. They include vulvas and vaginas in girls and women, and penises and testicles in boys.

Heterosexual: A person who is mainly sexually attracted to individuals of the opposite gender. Also known as "straight."

Homosexual: A person who is mainly sexually attracted to individuals of the same gender (boys to boys, girls to girls). Also known as "gay" (usually used for guys, but sometimes also girls and women) or "lesbian" (always women or girls), or "queer" (referring to either gender).

Incest: Sexual activity between relatives who are not allowed to marry each other.

Mandated Reporter: Any adult who works with youth and is required by law to tell police or child protection

agencies about child abuse he or she hears about. The police or child protection agency then must decide whether to (or is required to) investigate the report.

Molest: Another word for sexual abuse, often used in common language, but not a legal term or definition.

On the Stand: Where a witness sits to answer questions (usually when a person sits in the seat next to the judge in court) and tells his/her side of the story when asked. Each person on the stand is "sworn in." They must promise to "tell the truth, the whole truth, and nothing but the truth." After promising (swearing) to tell the truth, the witness is considered "under oath." Breaking that promise on purpose is called "perjury," and is illegal.

Oral Sex: When a person puts his/her mouth in or on the genitals of another person.

Panic Attack: A feeling of intense emotional reaction that includes dizziness, increased heart rate, sweating, intense fears or worries, and a belief that one is dying. This can occur for no apparent reason but is often brought on by a memory of sensation (smell, sight, touch, etc).

Penetration: When any object is placed (even a tiny bit) into the genitals or anal opening of another person. This can include vaginal or anal intercourse (placing the penis inside of the vagina or the anus) and oral sex.

Perpetrator: A person who commits sexual abuse and who is responsible for the abuse. Sometimes also called an offender or abuser.

Physical Abuse: When someone hurts another person's body to control or vent their own frustration or to punish him or her. Examples include hitting with an object or fist, burning someone on purpose, breaking a bone, or cutting skin. Physical abuse is against the law.

Pornography: Books, stories, DVD's, videos, websites or pictures of sex or sexual acts that are meant to cause a person to have sexual feelings.

Post Traumatic Stress Disorder (PTSD): A diagnosis given by a mental health professional that describes the way a person is reacting to a traumatic event that involved serious threat to the person's life or integrity. The reaction includes "intense fear, helplessness, or horror" during the event, and afterward being repeatedly reminded of the trauma through nightmares, intrusive memories, anger outbursts, physiological arousal ("fight or flight" reactions), etc. It can also include an avoidance of all things that remind the person about the trauma, numbing of the feelings and thoughts about the trauma, and isolation and withdrawal from self and others.

Prosecuting Attorney/District Attorney: A lawyer who is representing the state, and trying to prove to the jury and the judge that the person who abused you is guilty and should face legal consequences (state supervision such as probation or parole, required or mandated sex offender treatment, and/or time in prison, or some combination) for breaking the law.

Rape: Forcing a man's penis or other object into a person's vagina or anus. The legal term for rape is "sexual assault."

Sentencing: What happens when a defendant is found guilty of a crime and is sent to jail for a certain period of time or has certain conditions to fulfill (community service, parole, court-ordered treatment, etc.).

Sexual abuse: When an adult or bigger/older child uses a young person sexually, it is called sexual abuse. When any person bribes, lures, tricks, threatens, or forces a child into having sexual contact with him or her, it is sexual abuse. Adults or bigger kids may pressure a child into looking at pictures or videos of naked people or people having sex. Telling children sexual stories or taking pictures of children in sexual poses is also a type of sexual abuse. Touching children inappropriately or asking children to touch another person's private parts is sexual abuse. Some children are forced or pressured to have sexual intercourse with bigger kids or adults. Sexual abuse can involve parents, grandparents, Elders, uncles, aunts, brothers or sisters, babysitters, friends of the family, priests or ministers, community leaders, teachers, coaches, counselors, acquaintances, strangers, or just about anyone else you can think of. Sometimes physical or emotional abuse happens at the same time as the sexual abuse. Sexual abuse is against the law. The legal definition of child sexual abuse in Alaska is "sexual abuse of a minor."

Sexual body parts or private parts: In our culture, the parts of our bodies we think of as private and sexual are the genitals, the buttocks and anus (the opening between our buttocks and where the bowel movement or poop comes out), and in girls and women, the breasts. These parts are sensitive, and can feel pleasant and tingly when they are touched.

Sexual Contact: Purposely touching the genitals, anus, or female breast, over or under the clothing.

Sexual feelings: The exciting, pleasant, warm or tingly feelings that happen in response to an event (such as, for example, touching, talking in a certain way, looking at sexual pictures, reading descriptions of sexual activities, or watching sexual scenes in a movie). Sexual feelings can be triggered by lots of things, like seeing someone we really like, or receiving a compliment from a boyfriend/girlfriend. Human beings are supposed to have sexual feelings and sensations – it's part of our bodily structure.

Sexual Intercourse: When a male's hard and enlarged penis is placed inside a female's vagina. One or both of the individuals move their hips causing the penis to move back and forth inside of the vagina. Bodies have many nerve endings in the penis and vagina. Sexual intercourse is meant to feel good when it is done at the right age, with a loving person, under the right circumstances. If force is involved it can feel painful and scary instead. Sexual intercourse may result in pregnancy or sexually transmitted diseases (see below). When the penis is inserted into another's anus, it's called "anal intercourse."

Sexual Touching: Touching which involves the breasts, buttocks, and/or genitals and sometimes the anus. These are sensitive parts of our bodies, with many nerve endings capable of feeling pleasurable sensations. Sexual touching can include touch of any part of the body that creates a sexual feeling for the person who is touching or for the person being touched. For example, some hugs or brushes of the skin can be sexual.

Sexuality: A kind of energy inside that gives us joy about being alive and being in a female or male body.

Sexually transmitted diseases: A type of infection that is passed between people only through genital-to-genital contact. Can include gonorrhea, chlamydia, genital herpes, genital warts, gonorrhea, and HIV (the virus that causes AIDS). Some sexually transmitted infections can lead to infertility (inability to have children) or other serious damage if left untreated. They may cause pain, a smelly discharge, or have no signs at all. A physical exam can be important in detecting and treating sexually transmitted infections before they cause permanent damage or get passed to other people.

Sodomy: This is an old word that is still sometimes used to describe inserting a penis into another person's anus, also called anal intercourse.

Testimony or to testify: Testimony is the information that each person asked to speak to the jury will share. It's what you say when you are "on the stand." Sharing that information in court is called "testifying."

Urethra: The tube that carries urine from the bladder to the outside of the body. In males the urethra opening is on the tip of the penis. In females, it can be just in front of the vagina or slightly up inside the opening of the vagina.

Vagina: In females, the canal or tunnel leading from the uterus or womb to the outside of the body. Its opening is the middle one of women's three openings (in order from the top or front, they are the urethra, vagina, and anus). The vagina is one of the major sexual organs.

Victim Impact Statement: A statement written by you and/or your parent about how the abuse has affected you (or your family) and what you think should happen to the person who abused you. This statement is generally read to the judge (and jury if there is one in your case) after the abuser has been convicted, but before he or she is sentenced. The victim's impact statement helps the judge to decide what type of sentence the abuser should be given.

Victim: The person who was abused by the perpetrator, who has been hurt physically and/or emotionally, and who is not responsible for the abuse. In therapy and support groups, the person who was harmed by an abuser is usually referred to as a "survivor" rather than a victim. Since being abused does not define who you are but is one thing among many experiences in a lifetime, a more accurate term would be "the person who was abused."

Vulnerable: A state of being open in a way that allows a person to be hurt, but can also allow her/him to be open to healing.

Witness: Someone who will provide testimony "on the stand" to the judge and jury about something that he/she saw, heard, or has special knowledge about in relation to the abuse.

Index

INDEX

The NEARI Press

New England Adolescent Research Institute
70 North Summer Street
Holyoke, MA 01040
Phone 888.632.7412
www.neari.com

Assessing Youth Who Have Sexually Abused: A Primer

by David S. Prescott, LICSW (2007). NEARI Press. Paperback, 98 pages. ISBN# 978-1-929657-27-8

Current Perspectives: Working with Sexually Aggressive Youth and Youth with Sexual Behavior Problems

by R. E. Longo & D. S. Prescott (Editors)(2006). NEARI Press. Hardcover, 720 pages. ISBN# 978-1-929657-26-1

Enhancing Empathy

by Robert E. Longo and Laren Bays (1999). NEARI Press. Paperback, 77 pages. ISBN# 978-1-929657-04-9

Evolving Residential Work with Children and Families

by James R. Harris, Jr. (2009). NEARI Press. Paperback, 159 pages. ISBN# 978-1-929657-36-0

Growing Beyond

by Susan L. Robinson (2002). NEARI Press. Paperback, 216 pages. ISBN# 978-1-929657-17-9

Growing Beyond Treatment Manual

by Susan L. Robinson (2002). NEARI Press. Paperback, 42 pages. ISBN# 978-1-929657-15-5

Lessons from the Lion's Den: Therapeutic Management of Children in Psychiatric Hospitals and Treatment Centers

by Nancy S. Cotton, Ph.D. (2005). NEARI Press. Paperback, 354 pages. ISBN# 978-1-929657-24-7

Men & Anger: Understanding and Managing Your Anger

by Murray Cullen and Robert E. Longo (1999). NEARI Press. Paperback, 125 pages. ISBN# 978-1-929657-12-4

Moving Beyond Sexually Abusive Behavior: A Relapse Prevention Curriculum

by Thomas F. Leversee (2002). NEARI Press. Paperback, 88 pages. ISBN# 978-1-929657-16-2

Moving Beyond: Relapse Prevention Student Manual

by Thomas F. Leversee (2002). NEARI Press. Paperback, 52 pages. ISBN# 1-929657-18-6

New Hope For Youth:Experiential Exercises for Children & Adolescents
by Robert E. Longo & Deborah P. Longo (2003). NEARI Press. Paperback,150 pages. ISBN# 978-1-929657-20-9

Paths To Wellness
by Robert E. Longo (2001). NEARI Press. Paperback, 144 pages. ISBN#1-929657-13-1

Paths To Wellness en Español!
by Robert E. Longo (2001). NEARI Press. Paperback, 144 pages. ISBN# 978-1-929657-31-5

Promoting Healthy Childhood Development Today
by James R. Harris, Jr. (2007). NEARI Press. Paperback, 106 pages. ISBN# 978-1-929657-30-8

Responsibility And Self-Management: A Client Workbook of Skills to Learn
by Jack Apsche and Jerry L. Jennings (2007). NEARI Press. Paperback, 216 pages. ISBN# 978-1-929657-29-2

Responsibility And Self-Management: A Clinician's Manual and Guide for Case Conceptualization
by Jack Apsche and Jerry L. Jennings (2007). NEARI Press. Paperback, 118 pages. ISBN# 978-1-929657-28-5

Smoothies For The Brain: Brain-Based Strategies To Defuse Behavior Problems in the Classroom
by Penny Cuninggim and Shannon Chabot, (2008). NEARI Press. Paperback, 48 pages. ISBN# 978-1-929657-35-3

Strong at the Broken Places: Building Resiliency in Survivors of Trauma
by Linda T. Sanford (2005). NEARI Press. Paperback, 208 pages. ISBN# 978-1-929657-25-4

The Safe Workbook for Youth: New Choices for a Healthy Lifestyle
by John McCarthy and Kathy MacDonald (2001). NEARI Press. Paperback, 210 pages. ISBN# 978-1-929657-14-8

The Thursday Group
by PeggyElen Kleinleder and Kimber Everson (2009). NEARI Press. Paperback, 280 pages. ISBN# 978-1-929657-44-5

Try and Make Me! Power Struggles: A Book of Strategies for Adults Who Live and Work with Angry Kids.
by Penny Cuninggim (2003). NEARI Press. Paperback, 112 pages. ISBN# 978-1-929657-23-0

Using Conscience as a Guide: Enhancing Sex Offender Treatment in the Moral Domain
by Niki Delson (2003). NEARI Press. Paperback, 102 pages. ISBN# 978-1-929657-22-3

Using Conscience as a Guide: Student Manual
by Niki Delson (2003). NEARI Press. Paperback, 50 pages. ISBN# 978-1-929657-19-3

Who Am I and Why Am I In Treatment?
by Robert E. Longo with Laren Bays (2000). NEARI Press. Paperback, 85 pages. ISBN# 978-1-929657-01-8

Why Did I Do It Again & How Can I Stop?
by Robert E. Longo with Laren Bays (1999). NEARI Press. Paperback, 192 pages. ISBN# 978-1-929657-11-7

For prices and shipping information, or to order, please call: 888.632.7412
Find us on line at: www.neari.com